# How to achieve WEALTH FOR LIFE through Property Investing!

How to accumulate property, using little or none of your own money

ED CHAN

**www.chan-naylor.com.au**

ROAD TO WEALTH SERIES™

Published by
CNIP Pty Ltd
Suite 5, Level 2, 55 Grandview Street Pymble
NSW 2073, Australia
Phone 02 9391 5000
www.chan-naylor.com.au
First Printed 2005
This edition published in 2018



National Library of Australia Cataloguing-in-Publication entry

| | |
|---|---|
| Author: | Ed Chan. |
| Title: | How to Achieve Wealth for Life through Property Investing / Ed Chan. |
| ISBN: | 978-0-6482583-2-2 |
| Subjects: | Real estate investment—Australia. |
| | Saving and investment—Australia. |
| Other Authors/ | |
| Contributors: | Chan, Edward Sai-Ping, 1959- |
| Dewey Number: | 332.63240994 |

Typeset by Working Type Studio — www.workingtype.com.au

# About the Author

## Ed Chan

Edward Chan was born in Papua New Guinea in 1959. He completed his secondary and tertiary education in Sydney before becoming a Certified Practising Accountant. He began his career in the early 1980s working with PKF International and various other practices, but decided in 1990 to begin his own practice.

Today Ed is the Chairman of Chan & Naylor Business and Tax Accountants, which is recognised within the profession as being one of Australia's leading accountancy firms. It specialises in small businesses, self-managed superannuation funds and structuring of property investments.

Ed is a seasoned and passionate property investor and developer. His unique experience in working on the relationship between property investment and tax makes him one of only a few accountants who truly understand how to structure investments for asset protection and tax minimisation.

He has been a regular presenter at property investment and professional seminars held by the Institute of Chartered Accountants and the National Institute of Accountants in Australia. He has also been a keynote speaker at the National Directors' Conference of the Australian Taxation Office.

Ed Chan has had a profound impact on the way the entire accountancy profession operates, through the development of compliance systems and practices. He is a director of EknowHowAccounting Pty Ltd, which has a membership of over 520 accountancy firms around Australia that subscribe to the company's unique system of operations. He is also a regular presenter on best-practice methodologies to over 4000 accountants in public practice around Australia.

Ed has presented to over 20,000 people over many years on the merits of property, tax and structuring to protect your investments.

Ed lives with his wife and three children in Sydney.

**Also by Ed Chan**

*How to Legally Reduce Your Tax*

*How to Buy Property with Your Super Money*

*Small to great*

*How to turn your small business into a great Business*

**Ed Chan**

*Road to Wealth Series™*

**Ed's Dedication**

*This book is dedicated to my parents, who first started me out in real estate. Without your guidance and encouragement, this book would never have come to fruition.*

# Disclaimer

# Contents

# Introduction

This is not a get rich quick book. Contained in its pages is a strategy that can help you achieve your financial dreams.

What we're about to show you is a strategy you can follow for a whole lifetime. Therefore, whether young or old, this book has value for you and your future generations.

Much like our other books, it is written in a simple way and is intended to make you a "Player", only this time it's in the Game of Wealth.[1]

## MISSING EDUCATION

It's a sad fact that basic investing principles are not taught in schools. The current curriculum does not contain information on how to become wealthy, how to invest or how to understand finance. Basically, there is no method within our educational system for the everyday worker to learn how the game is played.

No matter what you are earning right now, or where you lie in the "classes", it *is* possible for you to achieve wealth for life. This book is the start of your educational process and your first step into the realm of the "Player", who is someone who knows how to play the game and win!

You see, we believe that:

1. Every Australian has the right to learn how to invest.
2. Every Australian has the right to services that help them implement what they have learned about investing.
3. The most effective knowledge is that which can be understood and applied.

---

1 **wealth**: an abundance of material possessions and resources.

That is why we have designed education in the form of books, DVDs and events that are simple, affordable and accessible for everyone who wants to learn more.

Becoming wealthy is a broad goal shared by millions. Such a goal can be achieved in many ways, most commonly by building and running a business or by investing (or both). When most people think of investing, they think of property or shares. While some of the principles in this book apply to any type of investment vehicle, we are specifically talking about the game of wealth through property investing.

And, like with any game, there are certain rules. Following these rules enables one to play the game. By not knowing these rules — or by playing with a different set of rules entirely — you aren't likely to have much fun playing. You can imagine the frustration of playing by the rules of basketball while trying to play football. If you didn't quit, then your team would soon grow short of patience and probably throw you out of the game. And it would be very hard to win football playing by the rules of basketball.

That's why Part 1 of this book is dedicated to dispelling commonly held myths about the game of wealth through property investing. Our game is one of wealth accumulation which means increasing your net worth; it's not a game of generating cashflow or making a quick buck. These are different games. They are not bad games to play and it's not that our game is better — the point is that they are *different*; they have a different set of rules. When playing the *Wealth for Life* game, we want to make sure you don't play by the rules of other games; we want you to play by the right rules, so you can win.

In Part 2 we'll explain our *Wealth for Life* strategy, answering all the common questions and "what-ifs" we normally get. Lastly, to prove that it can be and is being done, we surveyed several of our clients who were kind enough to provide their personal story in the Real Life Examples chapter. We hope you find these motivating and inspiring.

## ASSUMPTIONS

Throughout this book we've assumed the following:

| | |
|---|---|
| Property growth | 7% per year |
| Rental returns | 4% of property value |

Interest rates[2] 7% per year

When providing examples we've used the above parameters in our calculations.

To help you remember the basic rules of the game and to ensure you understand their importance, we've highlighted them and called them the "Wealth for Life Factors". These are summarised at the back of the book for quick reference and revision. Here's your first:

→ **Wealth accumulation is a game.**

These factors are what you use to help keep you on track and are useful armour against those who may try to discourage you or stop you. Use them as tools in your arsenal to make informed decisions on your road to wealth.

To aid in understanding, this book contains a glossary of terms used within the text. Words with a little number next to them will be defined in the footnote and can be found in the glossary. The glossary also includes other words that are not necessarily contained in this text but are there for reference when you need certain words defined as you continue your financial education.

As you read through, you will most likely discover there are some things that you will want to put into action. For this reason we've included a "To-do list", which you'll find at the back of the book. That way, when you think, "Hmmm, I'll have to check into that," or "I must remember to do that!" you will have one easy place to write it down so you won't forget it!

## NO VESTED INTEREST[3]

We wanted to make this point clear upfront: the reason we advocate property is because we like it as an investment vehicle or, more correctly, we use property as a means to achieve our investing aims. We make money running our business and we invest our money into property. We don't sell property to make money and therefore have no vested interest in advocating it. We've found through speaking to thousands of people around Australia, and even

2 **interest rates:** the percentage of interest paid on a loan.
3 **vested interest:** a special interest in maintaining or promoting something for personal gain.

in Asia, that people want to learn more about this strategy. We decided to put it in book form to make the information more accessible and easier to grasp. As property investors ourselves, we're keen to share this knowledge with you and hope that you learn something that helps you as an investor.

The one thing we can be certain of is change. Our economic environment is constantly changing and at a pace never before witnessed in recorded history. Therefore, it's important to realise that constant learning and study are the only real weapons against anything in life. Only one thing ranks as superior to knowledge and that is your attitude. Our philosophy is: never get too serious; life's a game, so have fun. That may seem strange coming from accountants, but hey, if we can do it then so can you.

Enjoy!

Ed Chan

**PART 1**

# Dispelling the Myths

# 1

# Your Role in the Game

We all need income to pay the rent or mortgage, to buy food and clothes; we all need income to live.

Income can be made in a number of different ways. You can sell your time or you can buy and sell a commodity for a profit. If you sell your time then you have a job (and there's nothing wrong with that, by the way). If you buy and sell a commodity then you're considered a trader.

Trading is often confused with investing because wealth can be achieved through both trading and investing. Confusing the two, however, can be disastrous. It's a bit like trying to be a dancer in a boxing ring — the two should be kept very separate! Or a Carpenter who builds kitchen is not a chef although they both work with Kitchen.

The word "trade" means:

The act or process of buying and selling; the exchange of goods.[4]

The definition of the word "invest" is:

To use money to buy something that will provide a profit or an income, or both.[5]

Note that the definition of investing does not mention "selling".

Therefore, the true definition of these words implies that an investor is one who accumulates and a trader exchanges items with another.

We are not comparing the two activities for the purposes of proving which is right or wrong. They both serve a purpose in society. What we're doing is

4 **Source**: *Thorndike-Barnhart World Book Dictionary,* Doubleday, Chicago, 1979.

5 **Source**: *As above.*

separating the two activities so you don't get confused as to which game you are playing. You can invest in property or you can trade property.

The Australian tax system, like others around the world, treats investors and traders differently. A trader generates income which can be taxed up to 46.5%. An investor, while they pay tax on income generated by their assets, pays no tax on the growth in value of their assets unless they sell.

Therefore, the first thing to realise is:

→ **A trader is one who buys and sells; an investor is one who accumulates.**

→ ***Wealth for Life* is a game for investors.**

The main difference between a trader and an investor is what they *do*. They both need to buy and often they both improve the asset somewhat to increase its value. But a trader has to sell or they make no money, whereas an investor has their assets make the money. An investor also tends to take a long-term approach and isn't fussed about minor dips in market value. A trader, however, is often affected by sudden value changes as these immediately affect the trader's income.

With such different viewpoints, it's easy to see how a person can get confused about what they should be doing — buying or selling? It all depends on which game you are playing.

We all, to some degree, play both games. We trade our time in a job and invest some of our salary into our home. So while you're playing the game of trading *and* investing, remember as you read through this book that it's written for you as an *investor*.

2

# Myth 1: The Property Market Will Crash

Newspapers are often full of comments such as this one:

**"PROPERTY BUBBLE[6] SET TO BURST!"**

Take a look at the following graph, which shows the growth of property prices in Sydney from 1990 to 2017. Added to this are the dates of certain media articles published with comments from experts regarding the property market.

As you can see, the doom and gloom of the property bubble makes a good media story but deals little in fact.

---

6 **bubble**: a risky or unreliable business or speculative plan, especially one proving to be fraudulent or unsuccessful.

## Media Articles Quotes Plotted Against Sydney Median House Prices

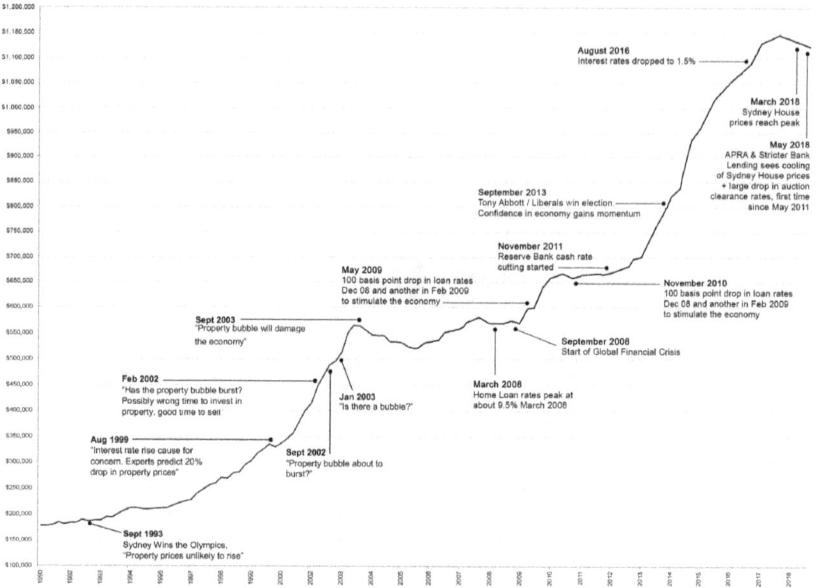


Source: Residex / Sam Khalil, Managing Director DPN.

## SEPARATING OPINION FROM FACT

We are bombarded daily with information regarding investing; as a Player, it's important to separate fact from opinion.

Fact = something that actually exists or has occurred.

Opinion = a conclusion or judgment.

The word "fact" originates from the Latin word *facere,* which means "to do". The word "opinion" derives from the Latin word *opinari,* meaning "to think".

As an investor, you first deal with facts and then make your own opinions. Don't make decisions based on the opinions of others as you are using their judgments as a judgment for yourself.

As we are passionate about helping others achieve their financial dreams, we meet a lot of people who are stopped or slowed down because they listen to and *believe* in other people's opinions. Some believe that lack of time or money is the main reason an investor doesn't succeed. This is not true! The

FACT is that most people don't succeed through lack of belief in themselves and what they're doing; their self-confidence is sucked out of them by others. That is what hinders most people. If you believe in yourself 100% then nothing can stop you. Nothing!

To avoid falling into this all-too-common trap, it's vital that you are able to identify the difference between facts and opinions and where they come from.

There are two types of people that offer opinion as facts. Clarifying who these people are will help you to identify them, so that you don't get swayed from your investing goals.

**These two types of people are:**

1. Those with a vested interest.

2. Know-It-Alls.

## THE VESTED INTEREST TYPE

Those with a vested interest in passing on the information to you have something to gain. The advisor to whom you are speaking will advise you based on the training they have had or the amount of commission they will earn. This may sound a little cynical, but if someone makes their living from advice based on commission, that advice might be biased.

This doesn't mean that everyone who is trying to sell property, shares or managed funds is lying or not telling the truth, or is twisting facts. What we want you to be able to do as an investor is to make an informed decision. You need facts to make a decision, not opinions.

What approach should the investor take? Only five simple steps are required:

1. The first step is to recognise when advice (or opinion) is being given as "fact".

2. If given by someone with a vested interest (for example, they make a commission from "selling" you their product) then realise the advice is liable to be biased.

3. Get actual statistics on the matter if possible.

4. Always work out the numbers with the full, long-term picture in mind.

5. Remember to look at the opportunity from the standpoint of which game you are playing. Are you an investor or a trader?

Once you've gathered all of your *facts,* then you can form your own opinion on the matter.

## THE KNOW-IT-ALL TYPE

These are the ones who know exactly what's going to happen, when the market is going to shift and why the economy is like it is. These people are easy to spot.

They *know* but they rarely *do.*

Usually they are full of advice of why NOT to do something, or possibly why you should do something different. They keep a good story or two up their sleeve and repeat it every time they see you. "Oh, I wouldn't do that. I once knew a person and when they bought a property ... oh my, what a disaster, blah, blah, blah."

All you need to do is ask them one question: "How many investment properties do you own?"

If the number is less than what you own, then don't listen to them any more!

These people are walking advertisements for their own fears, based on their own experiences or from listening to the opinions of others. Don't let their fears stop you.

This principle applies to any field. If you want to find out how to do something successfully, then ask someone who *is* successful in that area. Only then might you get worthwhile advice. However, even this is still opinion because it's their conclusion from the facts. But at least you know their conclusion worked!

Contained in this book are detailed statistics (facts) and our opinions as investors. What we want you to do is make up your own mind. Get all the facts first and see for yourself. And don't let anybody sway you from your course of action if it's working for you — not even us. Stick to your goals and your game as an investor.

- **Always check people's opinions against actual facts and make your own judgment.**
- **Take note of vested interests — does a person personally gain from the advice they give?**

## LET'S EXPLORE THE FACTS

What drives property prices? Obviously, it's supply and demand. If supply is low and demand is high, prices will go up; when there is too much property and not very many buyers then prices go down. This is simple economics. But what drives supply and demand?

**Supply is based on:**

1. The amount of land available in places where people *want* to live.
2. The number of properties being built in those areas.

**Demand is based on:**

1. The number of people needing a place to live.
2. The ability to get finance.
3. Affordability.

If you knew that 10,000 families needed a place to live and only 8000 dwellings were being built, then you could safely assume that with such demand, prices would increase.

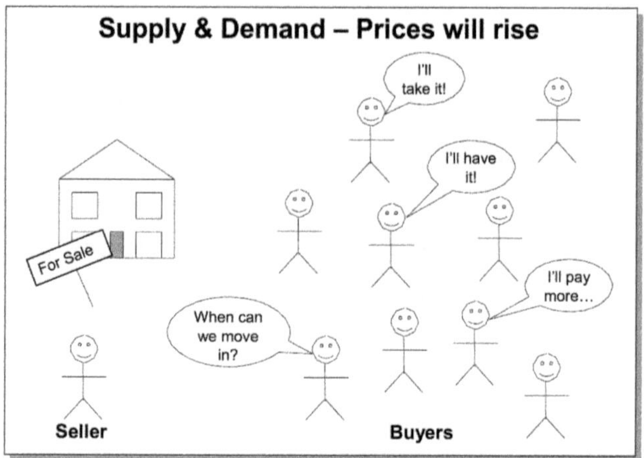


Therefore, one need only look at the above criteria, from 1 to 5, to determine what a property market is likely to do. If 1 is scarce, 2 is good quality and near shops, transport, work, schools etc, 3 is higher than 1 and 2, 4 is easy to obtain and 5 is reasonable, then you'd be doing pretty well.

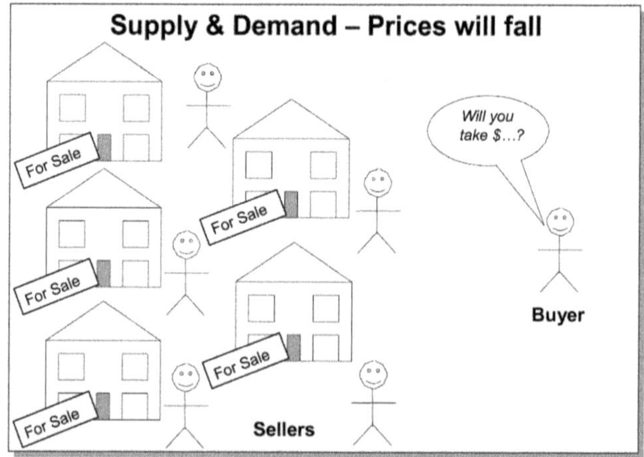


If any of the above criteria gets a cross against it then it might not be good, but that doesn't discount a possible future improvement.

## FINANCE

Another good indicator of the strength and potential growth of an asset is how much the banks are willing to lend against it. If a bank will only lend 50% of an asset's value then their confidence is only about half. If they are willing to lend 90% or 100% then they are pretty confident. And let's face it — a bank or lender has the resources to do a lot more research about the property market than we do. So we take the simple approach: if an *independent* lender will give you the money then it's a sign of confidence in the asset. An independent lender, by the way, is one not related to the asset. If you are buying property using the vendor's finance,[7] the prices could be inflated because no independent valuer has been required to value the asset.

- **An independent lender's willingness to lend is an indicator of their confidence in the asset.**

## UNDERSTANDING STATISTICS

Before we show you a host of statistics and graphs, it's important to know how they are calculated.

Experience has shown us that numbers can be twisted. The desired outcome can be achieved easily enough by being clever with numbers and graphs, but the results can be a far cry from reality (especially in our industry!).

Understanding the following fundamentals will not only ensure you grasp the information in this book, it will also arm you with enough knowledge to tell fact from fiction and truth from mere hope when you embark upon future investing.

## MEDIAN VERSUS AVERAGE

When discussing statistics, "median" means:

The middle value in a set of values that are arranged in ascending or descending order. It is basically the middle number in an ordered list.

Here's an example:

| 7 | 8 | 9 | 9 | 9 | 10 | 11 | 27 | 36 |
|---|---|---|---|---|---|---|---|---|

Median value

7 **vendor's finance:** finance provided by the seller of an asset.

When one compares this to the "average", which is the total of all the numbers divided by how many numbers there are in a given set, you get the following:

| 7 | 8 | 9 | 9 | 9 | 10 | 11 | 27 | 36 | Total = 126 |
|---|---|---|---|---|---|---|---|---|---|

Average = 126 divided by 9 = 14

Therefore, in the same set of numbers above we have this result:

Median value = 9
Average value = 14

When we're out looking to buy an investment property this starts to have significance. If you were told that the *average* price was $1.4 million then a $1.3 million property might seem to be reasonable for the area; however, this may not be the case.

Using the numbers above, let's assume that they represent property prices. The median price is the middle price for the area; half of the properties sold for more than the median price and half sold for less than the median price.

$700,000
$800,000
$900,000
$900,000
$900,000 — Median price $900,000, Average price $1.4 million
$1,000,000
$1,100,000
$2,700,000
$3,600,000

Using the average as a method of calculation to compare property prices has its flaws — one property worth an extraordinary amount for that area can inflate the average price. This is important for the investor because it could mean you are buying a property that is above the more affordable price within that area.

For example, if the property prices in an area are mostly around $300,000, then a million-dollar property is less likely to be affordable for people in that area. As an investor, rents for such a property would need to be about three times the rent of a $300,000 property. You can see how this might reduce the demand for that property. A good rule of thumb for the investor is to buy close to the median price for an area or suburb. You want to buy around the median price because that's what most people will be able to afford. The demand will remain high for property around or below the median price as shown by the following graph.

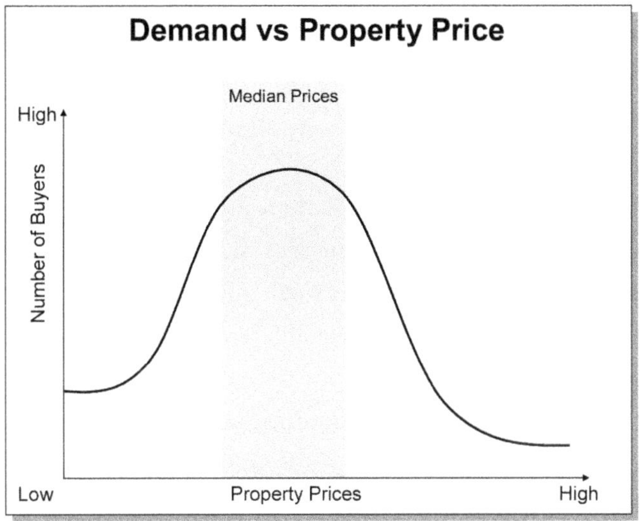


With this understanding, you can see that it's the higher priced properties that are likely to suffer the most in a downturn. Median priced properties are less likely to drop in value because enough demand should continue to keep the property value steady.

In times of economic hardship, people will still need to live somewhere but are less likely to be able to afford a higher priced property. Therefore, the demand shifts to the lower end of the market, as shown in the following figure. This is why buying around the median price in a given area is a good rule of thumb and is the key to point 5 mentioned above — affordability.

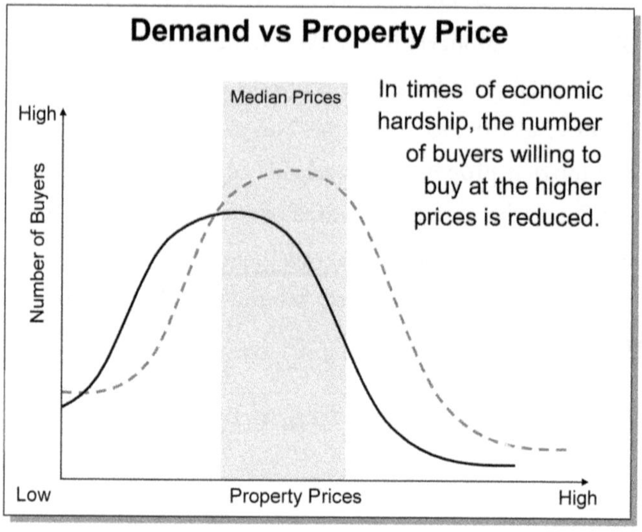


Another quick assessment is to ask three local real estate agents what the most popular price bracket is, in the area. It's interesting to note that the median price theory even applies on a smaller scale than a suburb; sometimes different streets within a suburb have different median prices. A good local agent would be aware of this.

The statistics used in this book quote median property prices.

## HISTORY

When it comes to choosing an investment vehicle it's always best to choose one with a track record. Future assumptions can be made from looking back at property prices. When you take a look at the following historical prices of Australian and UK property, it really makes you wish you'd bought more property earlier!

## Growth Comparison: Sydney & UK

| Year | Sydney Property Prices (Median) | Growth % | UK Property Prices (Average) | Growth % |
|---|---|---|---|---|
| 1942 | $1,665 | | N/A | |
| 1952 | $5,982 | 259% | £1,891 | |
| 1962 | $8,348 | 40% | £2,673 | 41% |
| 1972 | $18,528 | 122% | £7,880 | 195% |
| 1982 | $72,361 | 291% | £25,580 | 225% |
| 1992 | $183,215 | 153% | £50,168 | 96% |
| 2002 | $447,830 | 144% | £115,940 | 131% |
| 2006 | $520,300 | 16% | £165,035 | 42% |
| Source: Residex (Australia), Nationwide (UK). | | | | |

It's interesting to note that if you'd asked someone in 1942, "Do you believe property prices will be more than double in 10 years time?" they would have most likely replied, "No way!"

## Sydney Median House Prices from 1901 to 2006

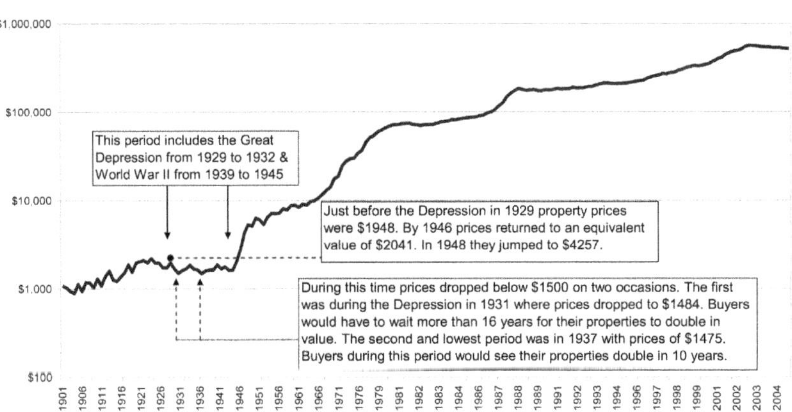

**Note:** This graph has an exponential scale. The column on the left increases at a factor of 10 times. This method is used to show the price movements in the early 1900s. The source data for this graph can be found in the Appendix.

You would probably get the same answer from someone in 1982, 1992 and even today. Just try it — ask someone and note their reply. It seems impossible to fathom that the median price will be double that of today. Yet if we take a look at the full available history of the market in Australia, the growth of property is evident. Even if we explore the effects of the most catastrophic events in our financial history, namely the Great Depression and the Second World War, we can see that property has still maintained its growth cycle. It took 17 years for prices to return to their pre-Depression high; if you'd bought at the bottom during this period, your property would have more than doubled in value in just over 10 years.

**UK House Prices Since 1952**

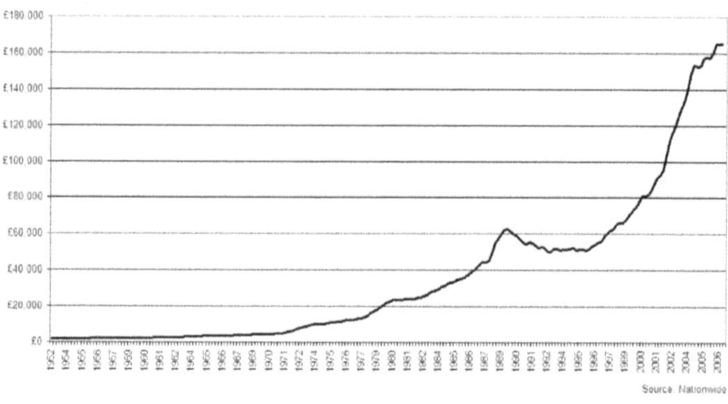


**Sydney Median House Prices from 1952**

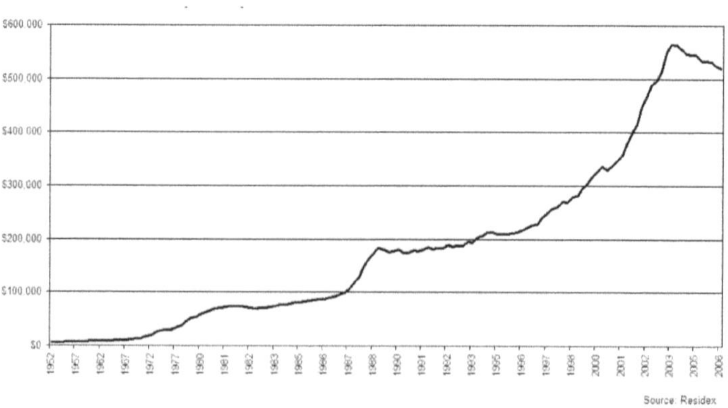

- **Median property prices in Australia have, on average, doubled every 10 years since 1901.**

Based on the above statistics, we take the conservative approach and assume that prices will increase, on average, 7% per year. This means that property prices will double every 10 years. Of course, the rate is rarely a steady 7%. At times it might only be 2%; it may even suffer a negative growth for a short period and then suddenly tremendous growth occurs. Regardless of these ups and downs, the Players look at the long-term growth, which we can assume to be 7% per year on average.

## ECONOMIC WAVES

Falling victim to the "Property Bubble" only occurs when the trend and cycles of the property market are not fully understood. One of the pitfalls a novice investor commonly falls into is the latest fad or craze. Emotion, fuelled by greed and the innate desire not to be left behind, creates the market peaks. These we'll call the Emotional Peaks.

This emotion, which drives the market above and beyond its "Actual Value", can soon turn into fear or despair and we then see a decline in the market. This decline is often encouraged by the media which, riding on the wave of fear and despair, publish stories that trigger the innate desire not to lose — so the novice investor then "gets out" of the market. Thus we get our next phenomenon, which is a decline below "Actual Value". This we call the Reactive Low.

"Actual Value" is a term we have coined which means the average between the Emotional Peaks and Reactive Lows. An investment, be it property or shares, is worth what somebody is willing to pay for it. In times of Emotional Peaks, that value is more than it was a short time ago; in times of Reactive Lows, the value is, of course, less than what it was.

Understanding the above, we can then see a pattern in the economic waves that affect our economy.

The general trend in the marketplace is towards an increase in value, fuelled by such factors as inflation, increasing population and the demand for infrastructure,[8] property, cars and food, etc. When the emotion of society as

8 **infrastructure**: the large-scale public systems, services and facilities of a country or region that are necessary for economic activity, including power and water supplies, public transportation, telecommunications, roads and schools.

a whole pushes prices past the demand, we then witness the "correction" and prices come back down. This is simply the dance between supply and demand.

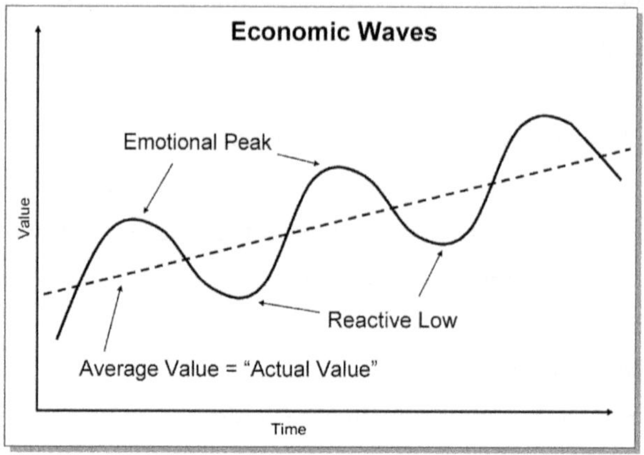


To some extent, regardless of when you enter the market, as long as you stay in long enough, your investment will grow over the long term. This is the principle of:

- **"Time in the market" is more important than "timing the market".**

It would obviously be preferable to enter the market at the Reactive Low stage instead of at the Emotional Peak. So how does one determine where the market is?

One of the key signs of an Emotional Peak is that everybody is talking about it. People who have never bought property before are buying. Suddenly, nearly everyone you meet is an "expert"! These things are definite indicators of a market being driven by emotion. Other indicators include: more buyers than sellers, auctions are packed with people and sellers are elated at getting a lot more than they ever expected.

The following charts, which show the property prices of Sydney, Melbourne, Brisbane, Adelaide, Perth and Canberra over the years 1980 to 2017, highlight the peaks and troughs.

## PERTH

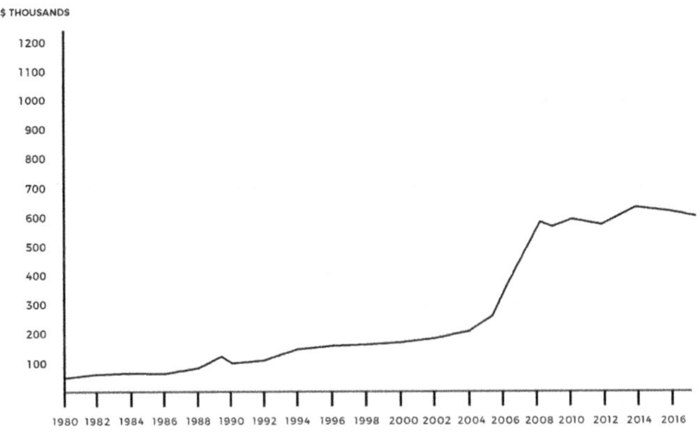


## BRISBANE

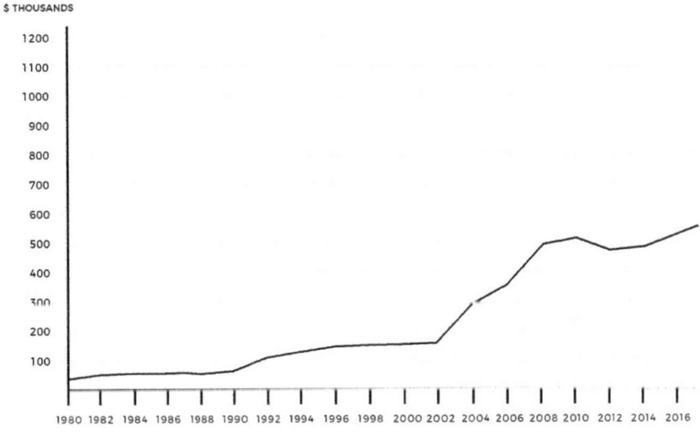

ADELAIDE

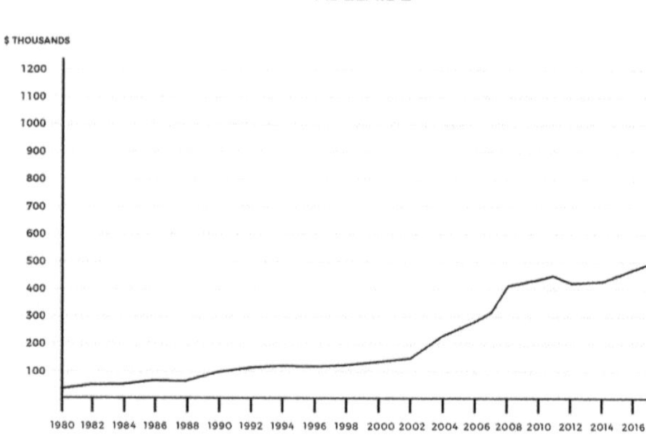


CANBERRA

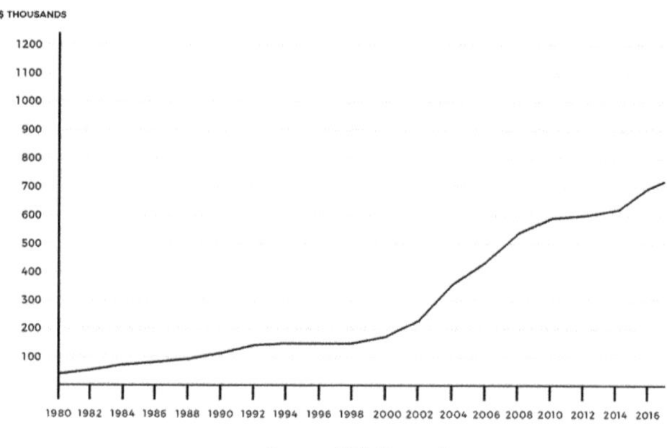


Source: ANZ Research

On the flip side, when the boom is over and prices start to level out and drop in certain areas, you'll see media stories of the latest victims — people who cannot sell and whose mortgage is higher than the latest valuation of their investment. Their basic problem is that there are more properties for sale than there are buyers. And so the market turns.

The share market suffers the same fate. Often it's a sector of the market that is doing well and then, when there are no more novices to join in the fun, the sellers outnumber the buyers and a decline occurs. A recent and memorable example is the "dot-com" crash of 2000 where, prior to the crash, the latest fad was anything to do with the internet. Despite such a correction, there are still some very strong and lucrative dot-com companies around that survived.

## All Ordinaries Index

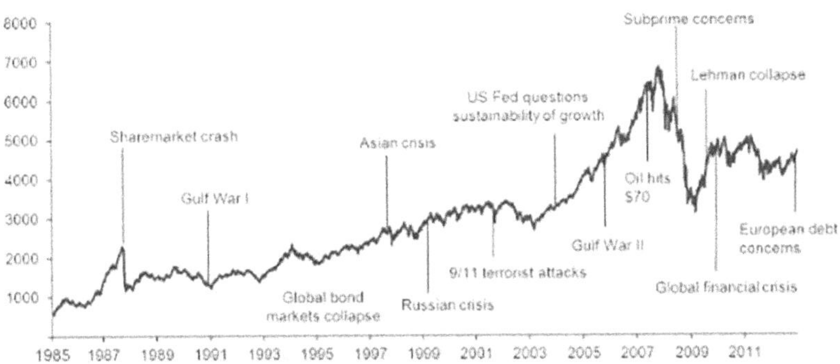


We can see by the chart below that the share market is more volatile than the property market, but the economic waves are evident nonetheless.

Source: Australian Stock Exchange.

## TIME IN THE MARKET

When one understands the economic waves and the principle of "time in the market not timing the market" an investor's skill or luck is not a prerequisite for successful investing.

A good example of this principle is the stock market crash of 1987. The All Ordinaries[9] dropped from 2238 to 1263. It took seven years for the stock market to return to its high of 1987. This highlights the principle above. Even if you bought in the stock market at the peak of 1987, and did not sell, your investment would have recovered from the corrections and made a return. Although your *timing* was poor, the *time spent in* the market corrected a timing error.

Again the stock market peaked around 2008 at 6400 and following the global Financial crisis it dropped to below 3000 and its taken 10 years to come back above 6100.

9 **All Ordinaries (often abbreviated to All Ords):** The index is made up of the share prices of about 500 of the largest Australian companies. Established by the Australian Stock Exchange at 500 points in January 1980, it is the predominant measure of the overall performance of the Australian share market. The companies are adjusted in value according to the total market value of their shares.

## SUMMARY

Understanding the principles contained in this chapter, the Player pays close attention to the supply and demand factors. And Players know that the property market goes up and down but they don't fret. Instead, they get into position, ready to play the next round!

- **Supply and demand drive property prices.**
- **Supply and demand are driven by the following:**

    1. The amount of land available in places where people want to live.
    2. The number of properties being built in those areas.
    3. The number of people needing a place to live.
    4. The ability to get finance.
    5. Affordability.

### Cycle

When demand increases either through immigration or economic factors it pushes prices up which then attracts Developers to build. When saturation is reached and they are unable to sell for the right prices the developers stop building for several years until the stock is depleted and demand once again increases prices which again attracts the developer to build again and the cycle repeats itself.

# 3

# Myth 2: Houses Are Better than Units

This is a common argument — that houses and land are better than units or apartments.

The theory behind this argument is that it's land that increases in value and because houses have higher land content than units, they enjoy better appreciation.

The idea holds some slight truth: land does go up in value, not the building. Regardless, such a claim is still a short-sighted look at the property market as a whole.

On the basis that land content is the key value of a property, then another way to express this argument could be "more land is better".

If this were true then a house in the desert, surrounded by miles and miles of land, is better than a unit near a major city. Of course, this is not the case; more land is not necessarily a better investment.

It comes back to what we have already mentioned — it's demand that drives property prices.

Not many people want to live in the desert and so land value in the Outback is not likely to appreciate as much as land in a metropolitan area where demand is higher.

Units and apartments, while they do have less land as a component of the investment, nevertheless enjoy good capital[10] growth in areas where there is demand for such dwellings.

For example, it's usually pretty difficult to buy a house in a highly populated area at a price that is affordable for the majority. Take Sydney, Australia, for example: It would cost a fortune to buy a house near the city of Sydney and if you leased such a property, the rent would be astronomical. This type of property would not be affordable for the majority of people and although it may go up in value, finding a tenant might prove a challenge, especially during tough economic times. However, a unit in this area is more affordable and therefore more likely to be occupied by someone working or studying in the city.

Therefore, the *Wealth for Life* factor that dispels this myth is:

- **Supply and demand drives property prices.**

And no matter if you are buying houses or units, your ability to borrow 80% or more on the investment is a good indicator of whether or not the bank thinks that the asset will achieve any capital growth. If you can borrow 80% or more on a unit or apartment then the lender believes in the asset. So, the following factor also dispels the myth that houses are better than units:

- **An independent lender's willingness to lend is an indicator of their confidence in the asset.**

## SUMMARY

Players don't mind whether their investment is in houses or units; they want property that is in demand with lenders willing to lend against it.

---

10 **capital**: wealth in the form of money or property owned by a person or business.

# 4

# Myth 3: You Need to Sell to Make a Profit

Please be warned! If you've ever sold a property then this section may cause you regret. The only reassurance we can offer is that you're not alone if you feel this way!

When those who have sold a property grasp the long-term view of an investor, they realise that they acted as a trader in order to make an easy profit. But by doing so, they switched games and this affected the speed of their wealth creation significantly.

You might think we're being dramatic, but this is such a common myth that if we added up the loss of potential gain for every investor who has erred in this way the total would probably count in the billions.

The truth is ...

▸ **Selling costs you money.**

Let's use a real life example.

We had a client (let's call him Phil) who wanted to pay for his daughter's university fees. He worked out that he needed about $30,000. Phil had an investment property he'd purchased some years earlier for $300,000 which was now worth $600,000. He contacted us to find out how much his capital gains tax bill would be if he sold.

Our reaction of course was to gasp at the thought of a client selling property, but once we got over our initial shock we proceeded!

We worked out the numbers.

Please note that the numbers within brackets are negative.

## Phil's Investment Property

| | |
|---|---|
| Purchase Price | 300,000 |
| Current Value | 600,000 |
| **Capital Gain** | **300,000** |

## Selling Costs

| | |
|---|---|
| Capital Gains Tax (46.5%)[1*] | (69,750) |
| Agent's Commission & Legal Fees (2%) | (12,000) |
| **Total Selling Costs** | **(81,750)** |
| Remaining profit | 218,250 |

The $300,000 capital gain was reduced to $218,250 profit after taking out the selling costs. This is before deducting the university fees. We asked Phil what he planned to do with the remaining profit. Phil's reply was, "I'll buy another property."

So then we worked out the cost of stamp duty and legal fees associated with buying the new property. These added up to approximately $25,000.

## Summary

| | |
|---|---|
| **Capital Gain** | **300,000** |
| Less Total Selling Cost | (81,750) |
| Less Stamp Duty & Legal Fees on the New Property (Approx.) | (25,000) |
| **Equals Net Profit (after All Expenses)** | **193,250** |
| **Costs as a Percentage of Property Price** | **18%** |

The end result was this: Phil would reduce his asset base by $106,750 (not including paying for the university fees). That means he would need to buy a property $106,750 below market value just to be in the exact same position — that is, a property worth $600,000 purchased for only $493,250.

Phil agreed that it might be difficult to find such a property so we offered him an alternative.

## BORROWING PROFITS

Although we're yet to dispel the myth of "debt is bad", we'll plant the seed now and let you in on a secret: debt is a way of accessing profits.

You need to factor in the added cost of interest and make sure that the asset will continue to appreciate over time. Nevertheless, it's true that debt is a way to utilise your capital gain. With this in mind, here's what we asked Phil.

"Why not borrow the money for the university fees?" The numbers look like this.

| **Phil's Investment Property** | **Kept Property** | **Sold and bought Cheaper Property** |
|---|---|---|
| Current Value | 600,000 | 463,250[2]Ⓐ |
| Current Debt | 240,000 | 240,000 |

| University Fees | (30,000) | - |
|---|---|---|
| Annual Interest 7% | (2,100) | - |
| Total Current Debt | (270,000) | (240,000) |

## Costs over 5 Years

| Estimated Property Price in 5 Years, when Daughter Completes University Course | 840,000 | 650,000 |
|---|---|---|
| Total Debt including $30,000 University fee | (270,000) | 240,000 |
| Total Additional Interest Paid on Uni Fees | (10,500) | - |
| **NET EQUITY**[3] $559,500 | - | **$410,000** |

There is a difference to Phil's Not Assets of $1 after 5 years and $225,985 after 10 years. Once we went through the numbers it was obvious that:

- **You don't have to sell to access your profits.**

Phil realised that selling the asset is like killing the goose that lays the golden egg. If you step out of the game, how can you continue to play?

We have found that:

- **As a rule of thumb, selling and reinvesting can cost about 20% of the asset value.**

We constantly remind our clients to do the numbers first. Always work out how much it will cost to sell an asset, including all taxes, stamp duties and legal fees, before you do *anything*. This is the application of the Investor's Sequence.

## INVESTOR'S SEQUENCE™

We first described the Investor's Sequence in our tax book (*How to Legally Reduce Your Tax*). It's one of those things that are so simple that hardly anyone gives it the attention it truly deserves.

Like a tradesman, the investor has tools — finance, property, research. These are all tools for the investor to *use*. A Player must realise that the *sequence* the tools are used in affects the overall outcome. Take the work of a tradesman as an example; it is much harder to drive a screw into a piece of hardwood with no hole already made. You can sweat and toil for hours on such a task. If one were to first drill a hole into the wood, driving in a screw would then be much easier. The effort and time involved is reduced by using the right tool first.

The Player who invests or goes into business should utilise their tools in a sequence that strengthens and protects the assets. The following diagram shows the most appropriate sequence for investing or starting a business.

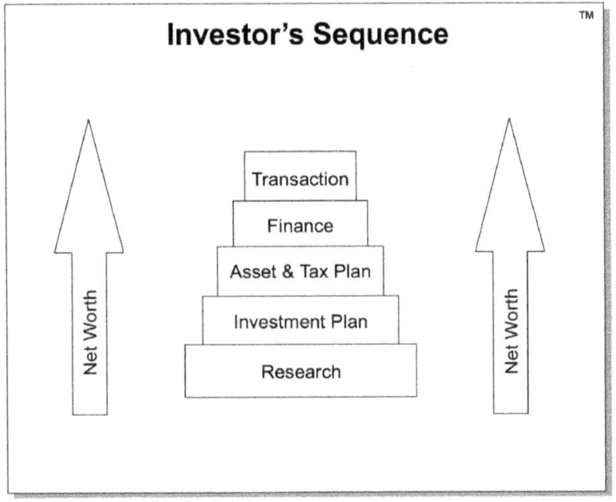


Each building block of wealth is self-explanatory. Before investing, you do your research, whether it's investing in a business, shares or property. Then you plan whether the investment is long term or short term. When that's all figured out, the Player then visits their accountant and works out the asset protection, tax plan and estate plan.[11] Only then does the Player organise finance and follow through with the investment transaction (buy or sell), or start business production.

It would be ludicrous to change the sequence and buy the asset, get the finance and do the research. This is obvious. Yet people will go ahead and skip the first three steps, which is just as crazy. In fact, missing out a building block is just as bad as doing it out of sequence.

And what we find all too often is this:

11 **estate plan:** a documented plan of how a person's assets will be taken care of after death. A will is part of an estate plan.

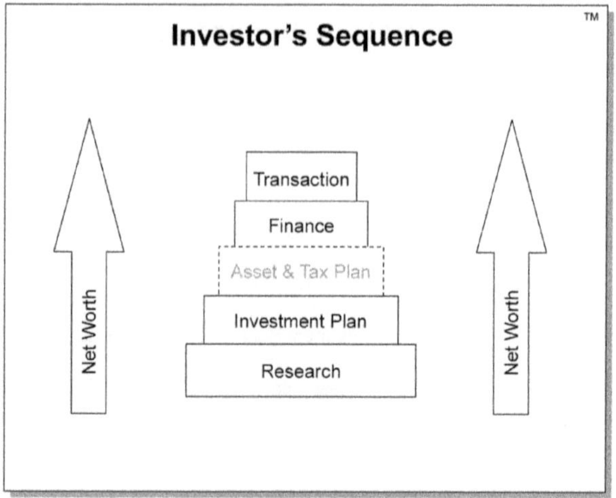


No asset protection or tax planning considered. The pyramid is weakened through this lack of asset and tax planning.

Instead, the accountant is consulted afterwards, usually at tax time. This is not a plea to visit accountants more regularly out of a desire to be considered more popular. (We've heard all the accountant jokes, you know!) It is much more serious than that because the result can be costly. Skipping a building block, like skimping on the foundations of a house, is not recommended; your net worth can come tumbling down. An earthquake can bring down a building whose foundations are weak; likewise, a bad financial investment or business deal, or getting sued, could be the equivalent of an earthquake. If your building blocks are solid then you may see it through relatively unharmed, but if any one of those blocks is weak, it can bring the whole lot down. The point is — doing it out of sequence can cost you money.

It is interesting to note that those we know who have done this out of sequence (and they are many) and missed the asset planning and tax step, inevitably end up having to redo the steps from tax planning on up, including refinancing and a re-transaction. (Transferring an asset into a trust, for example, is the same as selling the asset to the trust and is considered a transaction.)

The next most common scenario we see is this:

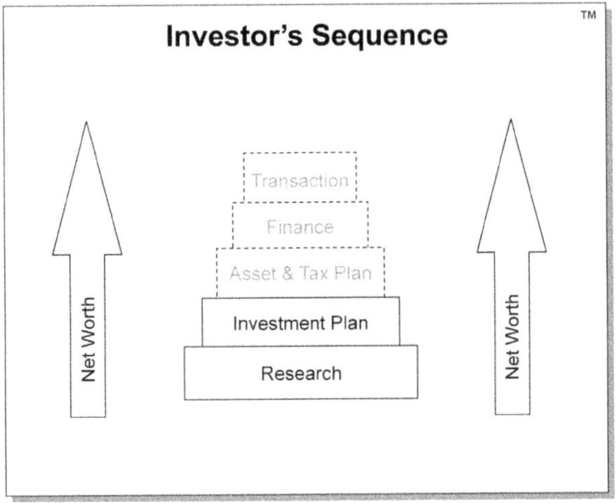


Lots of research and planning but no further action. It can be a little frightening buying your first investment or going into business yourself; however, one must overcome any fear and push right on through. The rewards are there for those who persistently pursue their dreams. You are the only one who really stands in your way. Just like a building is only ever built by *action*, block by block, with the end goal in mind, so too is the realisation of your financial dreams.

The Investor's Sequence applies to *every* investing transaction (or business establishment) not just the first one. And it applies to selling and not just buying.

Thankfully, Phil followed his Investor's Sequence before selling and learned that:

**►You don't have to sell to access your profits.**

## EXCEPTIONS TO THE "NEVER SELL" RULE

There are some valid exceptions to "never selling". These include such situations as:

1. A property is decreasing in value and not likely to rise.

2. A necessity to access all the equity (to pay for a life or death matter such as an operation).

And there may be others. If number 1 above is your reason for selling, be careful of acting on assumptions or opinions, as one person from our Real Life Examples did and later regretted (see Cherie's story). And in the case of number 2 above, explore all other alternatives first and always work out the costs of selling.

## SUMMARY

The Player doesn't need to sell to make a profit; they keep the assets and borrow instead.

5

# Myth 4: Cashflow-positive Property Is Better

By dispelling this myth, we are contradicting a great many investors. However, our point of view is — what would those investors be worth if they applied our philosophy?

Focusing on cashflow is playing a different game to building an asset base and increasing your net worth.

Take a look at the following scenario:

| **Investment** | **A** | **B** |
|---|---:|---:|
| Capital Gain | 7% | 10% |
| Yield | 4% | 6% |
| Total Return | 11% | 16% |
| Cash to Invest | 100,000 | 100,000 |

Which investment would you prefer, A or B?

Most people will tentatively say "B" as they know that it must be a trick question; after all, it's too obvious at this point which one is better.

Yet this is only half the picture.

▸ **Growth and yield are only half the picture.**

Let's factor in the ability to borrow. Banks only require a 10% deposit on asset A but want a 50% deposit on asset B. This means that with our available cash of $100,000, we can buy a $1,000,000 A asset and a $200,000 B asset.

Therefore, we get this:

| **Loan** | **A** | **B** |
|---|---|---|
| Loan to Value Ratio (LVR[4]) | 90% | 50% |
| Deposit | 100,000 | 100,000 |
| Debt | (900,000) | (100,000) |
| Asset Value | 1,000,000 | 200,000 |
| Interest Payments (7%) | (63,000) | (7,000) |
| **Cashflow** | | |
| Income (Based on Yield) | 40,000 | 12,000 |
| Cashflow (Income Minus Interest Repayments) | (23,000) | 5,000 |

Investment B has a positive cashflow of $5000 per year. But investment A costs $23,000.

Yet when you take the total of the combined capital growth and yield you end up with ...

| **Total Return** | **A** | **B** |
|---|---|---|
| Capital Gain & Yield | 110,000 | 32,000 |
| Less Interest | (63,000) | (7,000) |
| Total Return $ | 47,000 | 25,000 |
| Total Return % Based on Cash Invested | 47% | 25% |

The increased borrowing capacity has provided a better return on our $100,000 even though the investment B got a better return. That's why we say that returns (yield and capital growth) are only half the picture.

Let's explore real life examples of the A and B investments above. Asset A could be residential real estate because 90% borrowing is possible and many people can get that type of finance. What about asset B? What type of investment is restricted to a 50% lending? This could be a property located in a rural area or it might even be shares in the stock market.

This is why we say we don't care where we make our money from, as long as it's ethical, legal, safe and benefits the community in some way. What we do care about is how much we can borrow against the asset, because for us:

▸ **The size of your assets matters.**

If we could get a 90% loan on asset B, whooo! That would be great because we could increase the size of our assets and the return.

## WHY PROPERTY?

When you look at the overall performance of the stock market and the property market, they have shown quite similar returns over time. Of course, there have been stellar examples of individual shares and properties growing above the average market rate; however, over the long term, each market has generated similar returns.

The main difference is the fact that shares, in general, don't provide the average investor with enough leverage[12] (as in asset B in the prior example). Furthermore, if you do borrow money against shares, you can be subject to a margin call[13] if the shares drop in value. What this means is, as an investor, you are forced to pay back some of the debt if the asset falls in value. In this situation, you could be forced to sell when everybody else is selling. This is following the herd; Players go against the herd. (Of course, there are some lenders who provide 100% finance on shares without any margin calls; however, usually the interest rates are higher and there is a limit to the amount you can borrow under this arrangement.)

These factors don't make shares worse than property; they simply reduce the size of the asset you can play with. We believe that if you can start with a bigger asset you will be better off in the long run. Like our earlier example, a

12 **leverage:** investing with borrowed money as a way to increase gains.

13 **margin call:** *margin* in this sense refers to the capital or amount invested in shares. A margin call is when the lender requires a capital payment (cash) to maintain the required capital/debt ratio.

$1,000,000 asset with a return of 11% (yield and capital) will generate more than an asset worth $200,000 with a return of 16%.

To further highlight this point, here is a real life example. We had a client who was disappointed with her superannuation return after contributing $1000 every year for 25 years. She thought that she would have been better off if she had invested the money in property. However, this would not have been true if she had followed the *same* strategy. You see, contributing $1000 per year is building the size of the asset slowly. Our strategy is to *start* with a big asset. If you could get the same leverage with super and shares as you can with property, the *end* result would probably be quite similar after 25 years. The difference is the ability to start with a big asset and let it grow over time, instead of drip feeding it to make it grow.

Therefore, we simply want the biggest asset we can possibly get with our money. This is the fundamental principle of our *Wealth for Life* strategy — asset size does matter. That's why we don't compare the *returns* of different investment vehicles. What we want to know is how much can be borrowed against the assets because that will improve the returns on *our* money.

## SUMMARY

The Player knows that growth and yield is only half the picture and it's their asset size that matters most. They don't care what type of investment vehicle they use, as long as they can easily borrow against it.

# 6

# Myth 5: Debt Is Bad

This is probably the strongest myth of all. Don't be surprised if you struggle with this one. Many people work hard paying off their mortgage to achieve the great Australian dream of owning their own home, but that alone does not provide wealth for life.

The idea of having more debt is disturbing for the majority of people; most prefer to reduce debt.

This concept of debt being bad is brought about by the individual having to work hard to reduce their debt. High interest rates can create a situation whereby the majority of any payment towards the debt goes primarily to pay interest and does little to reduce the actual debt, the principal.[14] One soon regrets getting into the debt in the first place when the only way out appears to be working more hours, to earn more money to pay it off.

It's very disheartening working hard for several years and then realising that only a little has been paid off the actual debt.

Whether young or old, most people have suffered this fate, be it from high-interest consumer debt, such as credit cards and "interest-free" finance or simply a 35-year mortgage that doesn't seem to go away.

The word mortgage, by the way, comes from the French word *mort* which means "dead" and *gage* which means "pledge". Literally, the word means a "dead pledge". It initially meant the actual pledge was dead once the debt was paid off, yet for those stuck in the debt trap, it may seem like a "pledge until death" because they feel like they'll be forever paying off debt!

14 **principal**: the original amount of a debt on which interest is calculated.

So it's easy to see why many people believe that debt is bad. But there are two different types of debt.

"Dumb debt" is money that you borrow against something that doesn't appreciate, such as a car, TV, computer, holiday and, in general, all the "fun" stuff. These things don't go up in value; they tend to go down in value or are worth nothing once used (like a holiday).

"Intelligentdebt" ismoneyborrowedtobuyappreciating assets — things that go up in value, like property, shares and businesses.

Dumb debt should be paid off as quickly as possible; intelligent debt needn't be paid off ... ever! This last point you may have trouble with — the idea that debt can be left unpaid. Before we explain this in more detail, let's first grasp the concept that debt can be your friend.

## RETURN *ON* INVESTMENT

Return *on* Investment (ROI) is the amount you receive for risking your cash. Savvy[15] investors always get paid when taking a risk, whether it is profit from capital growth or an ongoing income stream.

The formula for ROI (as a dollar amount) is:

Sale Price – Dollar Investment = ROI as a dollar amount

OR

Annual Capital Growth + Rental Yield = ROI

The formula for ROI as a percentage is:

(ROI $/Investment $) × 100 = ROI %

When one is looking at the yield and capital growth, there are two ways to assess an investment. You can look at the overall performance of the investment (the total return) or you can look at the ROI — the return on the amount YOU put in.

---

15 **savvy**: having a sophisticated understanding, well informed.

Let's use property as an example. If a property grows at 7% per year and the rental return is 4% then we have this scenario.

| Property Purchase Price | $300,000 |
|---|---|
| 7% Annual Capital Growth | $21,000 |
| 4% Rental Yield | $12,000 |
| Total Return | $33,000 per year or 11% |

On the surface this looks good. Now let's look at the ROI, the Return on our Investment. If we put a 20% deposit on this property, then our investment is $60,000. Therefore, the ROI looks like this:

| Property Purchase Price | $300,000 |
|---|---|
| 7% Annual Capital Growth | $21,000 |
| 4% Rental Yield | $12,000 |
| Total Return | 11% or $33,000 per year |
| Deposit | $60,000 |
| ROI Formula ($33,000/$60,000) × 100 = | 55% ROI |

So while the property as a whole got an 11% return, our investment — our cold hard cash — got a 55% return.

This leads us to the following table, which highlights the fact that more debt equals a higher return on our money.

| **Assumptions** | |
|---|---|
| Growth & Yield | 11% |
| Interest | (7%) |

| **Investor** | **1** | **2** | **3** | **4** | **5** |
|---|---|---|---|---|---|
| Cash to Invest | 100,000 | 100,000 | 100,000 | 100,000 | 0 |
| Debt | 0 | (100,000) | (400,000) | (900,000) | (1 million) |
| LVR | 0% | 50% | 80% | 90% | 100% |
| Total Value | 100,000 | 200,000 | 500,000 | 1,000,000 | 1,000,000 |
| Gross Return | 11,000 | 22,000 | 55,000 | 110,000 | 110,000 |
| Less Interest | 0 | (7,000) | (28,000) | (63,000) | (70,000) |
| Net Return | 11,000 | 15,000 | 27,000 | 47,000 | 40,000 |
| **Cash Return** | **11%** | **15%** | **27%** | **47%** | **Infinity** |

As you can see, if you invest none of your own money at all then the return is infinity. That's because you can't divide by zero — try it on your calculator.

This example requires that you have an investment returning 11%, but regardless of the actual investment, the fact remains that if you can borrow more money against an appreciating asset then your returns are increased. Therefore, the *Wealth for Life* factor is as follows:

- **ROI is improved with *more* debt.**

**CAUTION:** Whilst debt can increase your wealth through beveraging, it can also increase your risks and losses, you need to take advice whether debt is suitable to your personality and ability to manage it.

## OTHER PEOPLE'S MONEY

Other people's money, or OPM, is a guiding principle for investors. If you take a good look at any Rich List, you see that they use other people's money, such as banks or shareholder investments, to fund the acquisition of assets. When you hear of multi-billion dollar acquisitions of businesses, or buildings and factories costing hundreds of millions, realise that people don't save their way to a billion dollars; they use other people's money for such acquisitions.

▸ **An investor should use other people's money before their own.**

But whether you've got intelligent debt or dumb debt or both, this principle dispels this chapter's myth.

▸ **Debt is only risky if you can't get more debt.**

It doesn't take a genius to know that when your credit cards are maxed out and you've borrowed to your full capacity, this is a dangerous situation. A sudden loss of income means that the debt can't be serviced.[16] But if the individual had a means to get a little money until a new income source was found then they would survive. In other words, if they could *borrow* money from someone until they found a job, they could continue paying their monthly bills. You may know someone who regularly needs to borrow money a few days before their next pay cheque — they are borrowing to service their debt or bad spending habits.

Some people have done this trick with credit cards, using one credit card to pay the monthly bill on another credit card that is due. If you keep doing this, however, with no assets to back up the debt, then you can get yourself into a tricky situation.

However, if you were able to borrow money, without any limit, could you afford the repayments on the loan? The answer is "yes". Of course, you're likely to say, "But how do I ever pay it back? I'll end up with a massive debt!" Yes, that is true, but the point we are making is you could go on forever and not need to pay it back if you could *keep* borrowing the repayments. In other words, if you had an unlimited loan account and could keep on borrowing, then you would never get into trouble. The way to achieve this is to have an *asset* growing *quicker* than the *debt*.

---

16 **serviced**: having met the minimum repayments required for a debt.

Of course, continuing to borrow repayments means the debt is increasing and you'd be paying interest on top of interest. It is this concept of debt rising and the idea of being in so much debt that is quite uncomfortable for some people, especially if they have been in the debt trap situation as described earlier. For these reasons, and many others, debt is rarely looked upon as a *tool* by the novice investor.

> **CAUTION:** A debt strategy will increase your risks if not managed properly.

## DEBT IS A TOOL

Debt is simply a tool to build wealth. And it is the most powerful tool an investor has. Therefore it needs to be fully understood and properly used.

As a tool, it's not dissimilar to using a hammer and nail to build a table. Those trying to pay the principal back to the bank are giving up their tools. What happens to your ability to build the next table if you gave back your tools? The ability to build wealth is dependent upon having all the tools (such as finance, property, structures, knowledge and action) available at your disposal.

This requires a shift of thinking for some people. A change in mindset is generally the first thing that needs to occur. We're not advocating that you borrow money willy-nilly and never pay it back. What we are trying to convey, at this stage, is that debt (whether intelligent or dumb) only becomes a problem when you can't afford the repayments. When you can afford the repayments then debt is manageable. When you feel like you **have to** work to pay the debt, then it becomes a burden. Hence, debt is not bad; it's the inability to *service* the debt that is bad.

We like to see our clients burden-free, and the first way to achieve that state is to realise that debt can be your friend.

## SUMMARY

A Player knows the difference between intelligent and dumb debt. Understanding this, the Player is not afraid of debt and uses it as a tool to ensure they can always service the debt no matter what.

**CAUTION:** A debt strategy is not for everyone and personal advice should be sort before endeavouring to use this strategy as you may not be suitable to it.

# 7

# Myth 6: Pay off Your Home Loan as Soon as You Can

Given what you've learned so far, we'll be a little blunt with this myth. Paying off your home is the worst thing you can do.

Before you put the book down, let us explain further. Most people have a principal and interest type of loan on their home. Often referred to as a P&I loan, the repayments are made up of a portion of interest and a portion that reduces the actual debt, the principal. Over time, usually 25 to 30 years or so, the mortgage is paid off.

If we were to take a typical example, here's what happens ... Mr and Mrs Detfre take out a $300,000 loan to purchase their $400,000 home. Paying it off over 30 years equates to paying $10,000 off the principal per year. If we take into account the value of their property doubling every 10 years over that period, then the picture looks like this.

| Years | Property | Home |
|---|---|---|
| | **Loan Type** | **P & L** |
| **Now** | Value | 400,000 |
| | Debt | (300,000) |
| | **Equity** | **100,000** |
| **10** | Value | 800,000 |
| | Debt | (200,000) |
| | **Equity** | **600,000** |
| **20** | Value | 1,600,000 |
| | Debt | (100,000) |
| | **Equity** | **1,500,000** |
| **30** | Value | 3,200,000 |
| | Debt | 0 |
| | **Equity** | **3,200,000** |

After 30 years, Mr and Mrs Detfre have paid off their home and now have a net worth of $3.2 million.

A Player, however, looks at it differently. Rather than paying the debt off, a Player wants to invest more and increase the size of their assets. Instead of paying principal and interest, a Player pays only interest. So the picture changes slightly to this:

| Years | Property | Home |
|---|---|---|
| | **Loan Type** | **Interest Only** |
| **Now** | Value | 400,000 |
| | Debt | (300,000) |
| | **Equity** | **100,000** |
| **10** | Value | 800,000 |
| | Debt | (300,000) |
| | **Equity** | **500,000** |
| **20** | Value | 1,600,000 |

| | | |
|---|---|---|
| | Debt | (300,000) |
| | **Equity** | **1,300,000** |
| **30** | Value | 3,200,000 |
| | Debt | (300,000) |
| | **Equity** | **2,900,000** |

At this point we look like fools because the net worth is better in the first scenario. But we haven't finished. The next step is to use the amount saved on paying off the principal to help fund the shortfall on an investment property.

Then we get this:

| **Years** | **Property** | **Home** | **Investment** |
|---|---|---|---|
| | **Loan Type** | **Interest Only** | **Interest Only** |
| **Now** | Value | 400,000 | 500,000 |
| | Debt | (300,000) | (500,000) |
| | **Equity** | **100,000** | **Nil** |
| **10** | Value | 800,000 | 1,000,000 |
| | Debt | (300,000) | (500,000) |
| | **Equity** | **500,000** | **500,000** |
| **20** | Value | 1,600,000 | 2,000,000 |
| | Debt | (300,000) | (500,000) |
| | **Equity** | **1,300,000** | **1,500,000** |
| **30** | Value | 3,200,000 | 4,000,000 |
| | Debt | (300,000) | (500,000) |
| | **Equity** | **2,900,000** | **3,500,000** |
| | | **Total Equity** | **6,400,000** |

After 30 years Mr and Mrs Detfre have a total net worth of $6.4 million from buying just one investment property. Realistically, the investor would accumulate more than just one property during this period of 30 years to build up a decent sized property portfolio. But this example highlights the point that paying off your home loan can cost you millions in lost opportunity.

## SUMMARY

The *Wealth for Life* factor that dispels this myth is:

- **The Player focuses on increasing their asset base, not on reducing their debt.**

**CAUTION:** This strategy may not be suitable to everyone and whilst paying off your home loan is not as financially sensible compared to buying a second or third investment property, many people benefit emotionally and physchologically from paying off their home loan.

# PART 2:

# The Wealth for Life Strategy

# 8

# Making It Safe

Now you're ready to learn the *Wealth for Life* strategy™ and for simplicity we'll refer to it as W4L™. It's important to note that this is not the only strategy available to the investor. There are probably thousands of ways to make money out of property. The reason we favour this strategy over others is because it's a passive investment method.

If you find yourself questioning the strategy, that's okay; it's likely that you still believe one of the previous myths to be true or, to put it another way, we haven't fully dispelled the myth for you.

If this is the case, we suggest you review the myth that is holding you back. If we have not provided enough evidence to dispel the myth, then do more independent research yourself. Get your own facts and figures. If you're still not convinced, that's fine; don't use the strategy! If, however, you are comfortable with it, then you can go for your life!

A word of caution. Don't confuse the W4L with your job or your current way of generating income. Although you'll see how W4L can provide you with an income stream, that doesn't mean you need to stop what you're doing. Rather, you should look at the W4L strategy as a place to put your money when you make it. If you enjoy your job or business then keep doing it. If you are a share trader and make money that way, great! The W4L strategy gives you choices and what you do with your time and how you make your money is your choice — so keep that in mind as you read. We are not advocating that you do this and nothing else.

## KEEPING IT SAFE

In our opinion, a passive investment approach should provide you with peace of mind and allow you to sleep at night. This is different from being a trader, with all the excitement and thrill of the deal. Our method is slow and steady. However, you could be aggressive with W4L and push the boundary, which is fine, but the most important underlying factor is:

- **Keep it safe.**

Safety is a personal thing. Some people feel very safe hang gliding or rock climbing while others don't. Our life experience, personality and knowledge determine to a marked degree our willingness to experience risk. A person is usually cautious the first time they do anything but through practice and repetition, one can feel more confident and comfortable. Practice and experience make it safe.

Most investment advisors look at the opposite side of safety — they look at the risk! "How does the investor reduce risk?" is a very different question to "How does the investor make it safe?"

You have most likely heard of the theory of diversification, which is spreading your money over a broad range of investments so that if one or two lose money, or don't perform, the loss is manageable because you've spread your money around. Diversification is the answer to "How does the investor reduce risk?" It doesn't make it safe; it simply makes it less risky.

Most investors are trying to reduce risk, which presupposes that risk must exist. Making it safe doesn't reduce risk; it removes it.

And because safety is a personal thing, the amount of safeness required is different from person to person. As you'll discover, it's you who determines the safety level of this strategy, not us. It's you who decides how fast you want to go. To use an analogy of rock climbing, to feel absolutely safe you might want three or four safety ropes, in addition to the main rope. Our view is that you should use as many ropes as you need to feel safe. W4L provides for such variations.

How can you buy an investment property and make it safe from day one? How do you factor in such things as economic ups and downs, bad tenants, interest rate rises or possibly losing your job? Most of these factors above are either ignored or explained as "not a problem any more". Professionals selling investments will often provide the investor with statistics and graphs to show how a situation such as "no tenants" is very unlikely to occur because of the current economic environment. While such information is important to have (because more knowledge improves the safety factor) it doesn't provide total peace of mind. Until now, no one has really provided the investor with a *solution* to these things.

We liken this to the weather. We know that in summer the sun shines and in winter it's cold and it rains. We also know that the weather changes and storms occur. And storms can do damage to the unprepared. How does the investor weather the storm and survive such difficulties?

The first step towards finding a solution is realising that these things *do* happen. Things can and do go wrong — the economy goes up and down; some tenants don't pay and can be a real pain to get rid of. Despite being the best employee, you can still suddenly lose your job through no fault of your own. Interest rates do go up and down. Like all human beings on this planet, the investor can have a bad day, a bad week and even a bad year — these experiences are part and parcel of life!

So rather than *hope* these things don't happen, or try to work out the possible risk of them happening and being happy with that risk, let's take a different approach and make it safe!

We don't like risk. We prefer that come hell or high water it will be okay and our families will be okay too.

And we create real wealth for life, safely.

▸ **The Player ensures they can weather the storm.**

# 9

# Wealth for Life

There are four basic W4L factors that need to be in place for the strategy to work. The first one is:

- **The *Wealth for Life* strategy works in areas where property prices increase over time.**

For this one factor to be true, we apply the following factors:

- **Property prices will continue to rise in areas of demand.**
- **The areas where people *need* and *want* to live will be in demand.**
- **Finance needs to be in place and constantly reviewed.**

That's it! If you can satisfy the four factors above, the only thing you need to add is time!

## PIECES OF THE PUZZLE

Explaining the W4L strategy is something we normally do face to face or to an audience at a seminar. In that environment, we can tell if our audience "gets it".

Describing the strategy in a book, however, presents a challenge because we can't tell if you are "getting it". Therefore, we'll provide you with bits of the puzzle so you can easily put the pieces together. And to make sure you're following along, we'll do a quick recap every now and then.

We've broken the "puzzle" up into three sections. The first explains the effects of property prices doubling every 10 years. The second provides examples of using equity to self-fund an investment property. The last section brings it all together by showing you how it's possible to live off your equity.

For those experienced investors, you might possibly grasp the concept early on. For novice investors or those who just hate numbers, we hope our examples and explanations describe the puzzle in a way that you can grasp.

It has been said that pictures speak a thousand words, so we've chosen several symbols to aid in understanding. These are:

| **W4L Symbols** | |
|---|---|
| 🌏 | Property Value |
| 🌏 | Debt (as It Is a Tool) |
| ? | Equity |
| W | Money or Equity Used to Buy Time |
| ? | Money or Equity Used for Lifestyle, Education, Holidays, etc. |

## SECTION 1: EQUITY GROWTH

We've explored the principle that property prices do increase, and for the purpose of our examples, we'll assume an average of 7% annual growth, which means property doubles in value every 10 years.

The following table shows the effect of property value doubling. The loan in this example is interest only and therefore does not reduce over time. Take a look at the equity growth over the 30-year period.

### Property Doubling Calculator

| Year | Property Value | Debt | Equity |
|---|---|---|---|
| Now | 400,000 | (300,000) | 100,000 |
| 10 | 800,000 | (300,000) | 500,000 |
| 20 | 1,600,000 | (300,000) | 1,300,000 |
| 30 | 3,200,000 | (300,000) | 2,900,000 |

While the property doubles in value and the debt remains the same, the equity has more than doubled every 10 years. This means that your net worth is increasing at a greater rate than the property is, despite the debt not being paid off.

Let's look at this in a different way and represent it graphically.

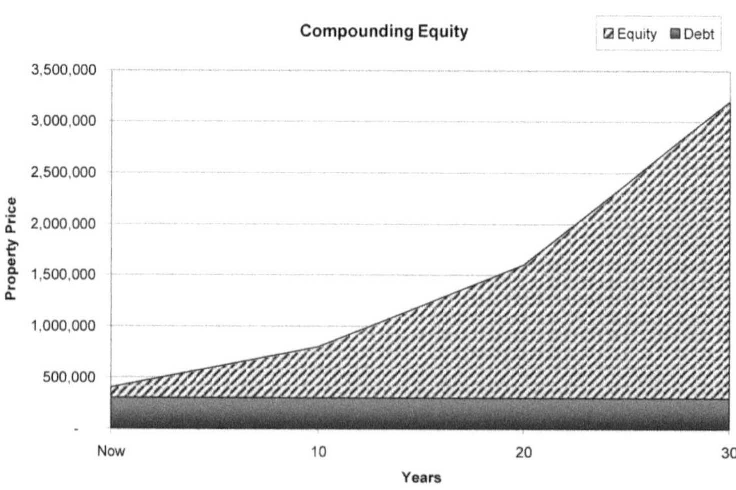

From the graph above you can see the increase in growth in the later years. This is why we say it's the size of your assets that matters. The bigger the asset base, the faster the compounding[17] growth. Look at the difference when starting with a $500,000 asset.

## Property Doubling Calculator

| Year | Property Value | Debt | Equity |
|---|---|---|---|
| Now | 500,000 | (400,000) | 100,000 |
| 10 | 1,000,000 | (400,000) | 600,000 |
| 20 | 2,000,000 | (400,000) | 1,600,000 |
| 30 | 4,000,000 | (400,000) | 3,600,000 |
| Download from www.knowledgecentre.com.au | | | |

Even though the equity position starts off at $100,000 (the same as in the previous example), the result after 30 years is $700,000 more in equity. This is why it's the size of your assets that matters.

## CASE STUDY

To further explain the W4L strategy, we'll use a theoretical case study of Paul and Sue, both aged 30. They have a lovely home worth $500,000 with a mortgage of $200,000 and having recently been to one of our seminars, now have an interest-only line of credit.

Their financial position looks like this:

| | | **Home** |
|---|---|---|
| 🌏 | Property Value | 500,000 |
| 🌏 | Debt | (200,000) |
| ? | **Equity** | **300,000** |

17 **compounding**: adding to the original amount, making it larger.

They decide to use $100,000 of their equity as a deposit towards the purchase of an investment property, worth $500,000. This makes up 20% and the bank is willing to lend them the remaining 80% of the property value. In effect, they have been able to borrow the whole amount of the purchase price.

So now the picture looks like this:

| | | Home | Investment Property | Total |
|---|---|---|---|---|
| | Property Value | 500,000 | 500,000 | 1,000,000 |
| | Debt | (300,000) | (400,000) | (700,000) |
| ? | **Equity** | **200,000** | **100,000** | **300,000** |

Moving 10 years forward, the property values have increased but the debt, being interest only, remains the same. Therefore, the picture looks like this:

| Years | | | Home | Investment Property | Total |
|---|---|---|---|---|---|
| **10** | | Property Value | 1,000,000 | 1,000,000 | 2,000,000 |
| | | Debt | (300,000) | (400,000) | (700,000) |
| | ? | **Equity** | **700,000** | **600,000** | **1,300,000** |

Paul and Sue now have assets worth $2 million and their equity has more than tripled to $1.3 million. They could at this stage purchase more property but we'll keep this example simple and see where they sit in 20 years.

| Years | | | Home | Investment Property | Total |
|---|---|---|---|---|---|
| **20** | | Property Value | 2,000,000 | 2,000,000 | 4,000,000 |
| | | Debt | (300,000) | (400,000) | (700,000) |
| | ? | **Equity** | **1,700,000** | **1,600,000** | **3,300,000** |

After 20 years have passed, Paul and Sue's property portfolio is worth $4 million. Their total equity is $3.3 million. During the next 10 years, their equity will once again more than double.

| **Years** | | | **Home** | **Investment Property** | **Total** |
|---|---|---|---|---|---|
| **30** | | Property Value | 4,000,000 | 4,000,000 | 8,000,000 |
| | | Debt | (300,000) | (400,000) | (700,000) |
| | ? | **Equity** | **3,700,000** | **3,600,000** | **7,300,000** |

In summary, by buying just one investment property, Paul and Sue have accumulated a total of $8 million in property value over 30 years. Taking away their $700,000 debt means they have $7.3 million in equity.

During the course of those 30 years, Paul and Sue had to pay the interest on their debt and expenses relating to the property. Of course, they would have received rental income and tax benefits from having the investment property, but nevertheless they would have needed to make up the shortfall — and most investors do that from their own salary.

# SECTION 2: SELF-FUNDING INVESTMENT PROPERTY

## WHAT MAKES IT SAFE?

Having access to money helps you to weather the storm and ride the economic waves. What makes it safe is being able to continually *service* debt repayments.

The key to an investment being safe is that you don't rely on your income to service the debt. If an investment could pay for itself and didn't need any money from you, would that make it easier for you? The answer of course is, "Yes!"

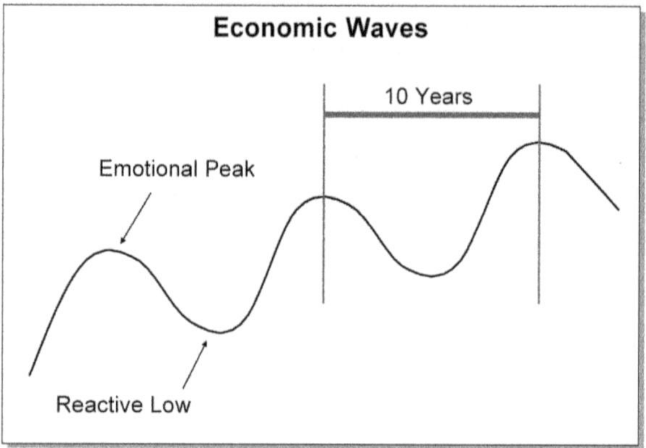


The key factor is weathering the storm — having the ability to last until the next property wave. Looking at the property cycle, we know we need to be able to last 10 years because the time frame from peak to peak is normally 7 to 10 years. Depending on when you bought in the cycle, you could have less than 10 years until the next boom. But we like to be conservative (surprise, surprise) so 10 years is our yardstick.

The focus for the investor then becomes, "Can I last 10 years?" By asking this question, the focus has changed from property and money to *time*. What the Player is interested in is, "How long can I last?" The main yardstick for the Player is TIME.

- ***Wealth for Life*** **is not about buying real estate, it's about *buying time.***

For it to be safe, you must be able to buy 10 years of time.

## THE COST OF BUYING TIME

An investment property has associated costs, such as interest payments, repairs and rates to name a few. It also makes a rental income and has tax benefits relating to negative gearing and depreciation.

The shortfall of these is the annual holding cost. This can be roughly calculated to be 2% of the purchase price for an investment property with 100% finance. This is a typical scenario when using the existing equity in your home for a deposit and borrowing the rest.

The table below shows how this 2% holding cost is calculated. Of course, the figures may vary depending on the specific property, taxable income, proportion of finance and the economic environment, but it is a good yardstick.

### Annual Holding Cost Assumptions

| | **% (of purchase price)** |
|---|---|
| Interest Rate | (7%) |
| Expenses | (1%) |
| Yield (Rent) | 4% |
| Tax Benefits | 2% |
| **Total** | **(2%)** |
| Note: Stamp duty and legal costs have not being included in this calculation. Interest rate calculation for 100% financed property. | |

This is only a calculation of the initial holding cost and will change over time as the rental income increases to become positively geared (after five to seven years). But, as we've already mentioned, what makes it safe is the ability to *buy time* and this should be the main focus of the investor.

So we will assume (worst case scenario) that the rents won't increase and the property will always cost 2% per year to hold. This holding cost is usually funded by the investor from their salary. The question is, "How do we make it safe?"

Let's have another look at when Paul and Sue first bought their investment property.

## Paul and Sue Starting Out

| | | Home | Investment Property | Total |
|---|---|---|---|---|
| 🌏 | Property Value | 500,000 | 500,000 | 1,000,000 |
| 🌏 | Debt | (300,000) | (400,000) | (700,000) |
| ? | **Equity** | **200,000** | **100,000** | **300,000** |

Paul and Sue used $100,000 from the equity on their home plus the $400,000 they borrowed to buy their $500,000 investment property making it, in effect, 100% financed. Therefore, their investment property would cost Paul and Sue about $10,000 (2% of $500,000) a year to hold.

To make it safe, is it possible to pay the holding cost from their available equity? Would they be able to last 10 years until their property doubled in value?

A simple calculation is $10,000 per year for 10 years equals $100,000. That seems feasible as their total equity at this point is $300,000. But in addition to this, we would need to take into account the interest charged on the use of that equity. This requires that you understand the concept of capitalising interest.

## CAPITALISING INTEREST

Capitalising, in finance terms, is using debt as capital. Interest on a loan is normally paid from existing capital (like cash in your back pocket), but by capitalising the expense, we are using debt to pay for debt, so you make no payment but let the loan balance gradually rise. In essence, we're borrowing money (cash) to pay for the interest. This is like withdrawing $100 from your credit card to pay the monthly credit card bill. The following diagram describes the flow.

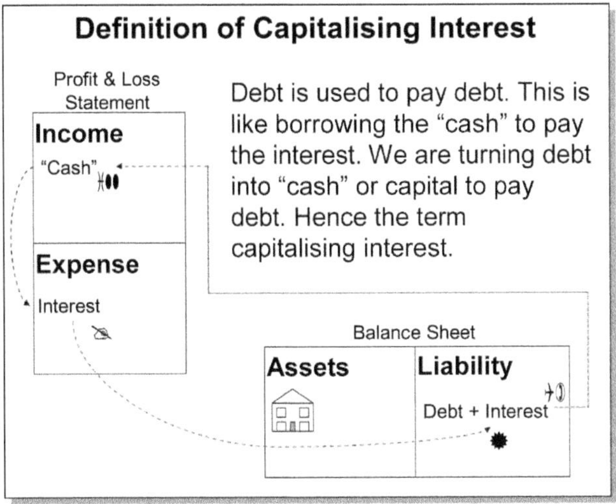


What the Player needs to understand is the *long-term effect* of capitalising interest. Borrowing money to service debt needs to be monitored and planned beforehand. Keeping in mind the W4L principle of buying time, what the Player must ensure when using *any* equity is that they can still last until the next property cycle.

The following diagram shows how debt increases when capitalising your interest. As you can see, instead of paying the interest on the debt, you are adding it onto your debt; in effect, you are borrowing to fund the interest payment.

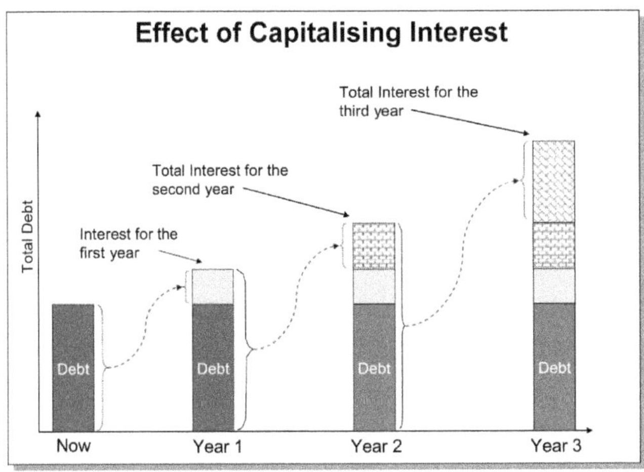


Notice that the interest compounds, as you are charged interest on the interest that you borrow. Therefore, the growth of the debt needs to be less than the growth of the property. Or, to put it another way, the property value must grow faster than the debt.

Although an obvious statement, it is violation of this principle that leads many home owners and investors into trouble. If, for example, Paul and Sue decided to spend all of their available equity on a holiday, what they would have done is spend their "time buffer". Then the only method of servicing the debt would be from their salary. This is how people fall into the debt trap. When in this situation, the solution most people look for is to increase their income, which usually means more responsibility and more working hours.

A Player, on the other hand, understands this basic principle and knows that all that is required is factoring the interest component into their calculations to make sure they have enough of a buffer to weather the storm. The Player realises that equity is *first* used to buy time — not holidays, cars or toys.

Now, let's look at the result of using the equity of an investment property to cover its holding costs and capitalise the interest on the equity so used. This way, you wouldn't need to pay anything out of your own pocket. We have put it in the form of a table and will first explain each column to ensure you follow.

**Year:** This is the number of years since the property purchase. The figures in the subsequent columns correspond to that year.

**Property value:** The property value at the start of the year.

**Debt:** The total debt at the start of that year, including equity used to pay holding costs and compounding interest.

**Equity:** Property value less the debt.

**Holding costs:** The cost of holding on to the property, which is normally paid from salary. In this example, this cost is paid using the equity of the property and can be looked upon as buying time, hence the use of the W symbol.

**Interest:** The annual compounding interest on the equity used.

**Equity used:** This is the total equity used so far. It includes the equity used for the holding costs plus the capitalised interest on that equity.

**WARNING:** Using Debt to Fund debt is risky and should only be considered after seeking financial advice.

## Self-funding Calculator — Annual Period

| Year | Property Value | Debt | ? Equity | W Holding Costs 2% | Interest 7% | Equity Used |
|---|---|---|---|---|---|---|
| Now | 500,000 | (400,000) | 100,000 | (10,000) | (700) | (10,700) |
| 1 | 535,000 | (410,700) | 124,300 | (10,000) | (1,449) | (22,149) |
| 2 | 572,450 | (422,149) | 150,301 | (10,000) | (2,250) | (34,399) |
| 3 | 612,522 | (434,399) | 178,122 | (10,000) | (3,108) | (47,507) |
| 4 | 655,398 | (447,507) | 207,891 | (10,000) | (4,026) | (61,533) |
| 5 | 701,276 | (461,533) | 239,743 | (10,000) | (5,007) | (76,540) |
| 6 | 750,365 | (476,540) | 273,825 | (10,000) | (6,058) | (92,598) |
| 7 | 802,891 | (492,598) | 310,293 | (10,000) | (7,182) | (109,780) |
| 8 | 859,093 | (509,780) | 349,313 | (10,000) | (8,385) | (128,164) |
| 9 | 919,230 | (528,164) | 391,065 | (10,000) | (9,672) | (147,836) |
| 10 | 983,576 | (547,836) | 435,740 | | | |
| **Total** | | | | **(100,000)** | **(47,836)** | **(147,836)** |
| Assumptions: Rental income will NOT increase over the 10-year period and interest rates will stay the same. | | | | | | |

A point worth highlighting is that despite the debt increasing, the equity has increased even more. The debt has increased $147,836 over the 10 years yet the equity has increased by over $335,000.

The above could be achieved without using any personal income; the property is funding itself. As an investor, this makes it safe because you no longer have to rely solely on your salary or the tenant paying rent.

At this point, you might be concerned about the detail. What if the property doesn't double in 10 years? What if the interest rates are higher? What if the property is vacant? What if, what if, what if ...?

Right now, the answer is: don't focus on the detail, focus instead on the BIG PICTURE. If you understand the big picture concept, we'll show you how to take care of the detail.

Reviewing the above table, you can see how it's possible to use your equity to self-fund the investment property. Because we're dealing with numbers and averages you could say, "It doesn't work that way in real life." And you'd be right.

The truth is that property rarely increases at a steady rate, which is why we always take a long-term view of 10 years. Also, you need to build in safety nets to ensure you are 100% comfortable. That's why we assume the worst case scenario and say the property will cost $10,000 every year.

**WARNING**: If the banks changed their lending policies and they do that from time to time it could have a dine effect on this strategy.

## Quick Recap

Let's do a quick recap. At this stage you have seen that property values double every 10 years (based on historical performance) and we've shown you how equity can more than double despite not paying off any debt. You've also seen how an investment property could be self-funded, using the equity as it grows over time. The next phase is how, starting with your own home, you can build a self-funding property portfolio.

## COST OF USING EQUITY

In Australia, the highest income tax rate is 46.5% and GST is 10%. Using your equity is, however, tax free. But there is the *cost* of *money* to consider. When you use (borrow) money, you pay interest, but only when you use it. The interest you pay could be considered a sort of tax — which in our current environment is less than the cost of GST!

In our last table, we showed the costs involved with a self-funded investment over a 10-year period. The end result was:

## Self-funding Calculator — Annual Period

| Year | Property Value | Debt | ? Equity | W Holding Costs 2% | Interest 7% | Equity Used |
|---|---|---|---|---|---|---|
| 10 | 983,576 | (547,836) | 435,740 | | | |
| **Total** | | | | **(100,000)** | **(47,836)** | **(147,836)** |
| Assumptions: Rental income will NOT increase over the 10-year period and interest rates will stay the same. | | | | | | |

The calculator above shows that by capitalising the interest payments on the holding costs, the interest has compounded over the 10 years to a total interest charge of $47,836.

Paying the interest of $47,836 is the cost of using the equity; it's a bit like a tax. To help identify this cost clearly, we coined the term "Equity Charge"™, which is the accumulated capitalised interest on the equity used, over a specified period. To keep the calculation simple, we've designed an easy to use calculator specifically for the purpose of working out Equity Charge™.

## EQUITY CHARGE™ CALCULATOR

This makes it very easy to work out how much equity you will use as you implement the *Wealth for Life* strategy. We have used it to calculate the figures for the remainder of the examples in this book.

As you can see, the results match our earlier calculations.

| **Equity Charge Calculator** | | | |
|---|---|---|---|
| Number of Years (Buying Time) | | 10 | years |
| Annual Holding Cost | $ | 10,000 | |
| Annual Lifestyle Cost | $ | | |
| Amount of Equity Already Used | $ | | |
| Annual Interest Rate | | 7.00% | |
| **Prediction for the next 10 years** | | | |
| Holding Costs | $ | 100,000 | |
| Lifestyle Costs | $ | - | |
| Equity Charge™ | $ | 47,836 | |
| Total Equity Required | $ | 147,836 | |

It's important to monitor this expense, otherwise it could get out of hand and the debt could increase faster than the value of the property. However, if you are following a sensible strategy, you simply factor it in and make sure you have enough of a buffer.

Using this calculator, we can now work out the total amount of capitalised interest on the holding costs over a specified time period and hence the total amount of equity used when self-funding an investment property.

## BUYING TIME

Let's now go back to Paul and Sue, who are eager to find out if they can afford to self-fund their property or whether they need to use some of their salary.

### Paul and Sue Starting Out

| | | **Home** | **Investment Property** | **Total** |
|---|---|---|---|---|
| 🌏 | Property Value | 500,000 | 500,000 | 1,000,000 |
| 🌏 | Debt | (300,000) | (400,000) | (700,000) |
| ? | **Equity** | **200,000** | **100,000** | **300,000** |

With $300,000 in equity and understanding the principle of buying time, we want to make sure they will last at least 10 years.

We already know that the holding cost on their $500,000 investment property is $10,000 (2%) a year and, using the Equity Calculator (and rounding off the numbers for simplicity), we have determined that it will require $148,000 in equity for the first 10 years.

| | **Self-funding Costs for the First 10 Years** | |
|---|---|---|
| W | Holding Costs | (100,000) |
| W | Equity Charge on Holding Costs | (48,000) |
| | **Total Equity Required** | **(148,000)** |

With $300,000 of available equity, the question is: Can they last 10 years if they use $148,000 of their equity to fund the investment property? The answer is “Yes!”, because they are still left with $152,000 in equity. So, of course, they go ahead!

Now, 10 years later, the property values have doubled and the picture looks like this:

| Years | | | Total Portfolio |
|---|---|---|---|
| 10 | 🌏 | Property Value | 2,000,000 |
| | 🌏 | Initial Debt | (700,000) |
| | W | Less Holding Costs | (100,000) |
| | W | Less Equity Charge | (48,000) |
| | ? | **Total Remaining Equity** | **1,152,000** |

Over the 10-year period, Paul and Sue managed to increase their equity from $300,000 to $1.152 million and were able to do so without using any of their own money. The summary table below clearly shows their position after 10 years.

| Years | Summary | | Total Portfolio |
|---|---|---|---|
| 10 | 🌏 | Property Value | 2,000,000 |
| | 🌏 | Initial Debt | (700,000) |
| | W | Equity Used | (148,000) |
| | ? | **Equity** | **1,152,000** |

This has provided Paul and Sue with *choices*. In essence, they have saved $10,000 of their salary a year. There is nothing stopping them funding more investment property with that $10,000. They know, no matter what, that the investment can pay for itself. Remember, the property may well become cashflow-positive during those 10 years. But, regardless, what has been achieved is a buffer. They know they can weather the storm; even if they lose their jobs, the holding costs and interest can still be paid from their equity.

This often requires quite a significant shift in thinking. By using debt as a *tool,* Paul and Sue were able to buy an investment property and didn't need *any* of their own money to do so.

Now let's take a look at the next 10 years and assume that the property will still cost $10,000 per year to self-fund from their equity. How will that affect their overall equity growth?

Using the Equity Charge Calculator, we can determine the Equity Charge on the next 10 years of holding costs as well as on the amount of equity used so far (which is $148,000).

| **Equity Charge™ Calculator** | | | |
|---|---|---|---|
| Number of Years (Buying Time) | | 10 | years |
| Annual Holding Cost | $ | 10,000 | |
| Annual Lifestyle Cost | $ | | |
| Amount of Equity Already Used | $ | 148,000 | |
| Annual Interest Rate | | 7.00% | |
| **Prediction for the next 10 years** | | | |
| Holding Costs | $ | 100,000 | |
| Lifestyle Costs | $ | - | |
| Equity Charge™ | $ | 190,974 | |
| Total Equity Required | $ | 290,974 | |

With $1,152,000 of available equity, they can more than cover the $290,000 of equity required to continue to self-fund their property for another 10 years.

Fast forward another 10 years, taking us to the 20th year of investing, and the picture looks like this:

| Years | | | Total Portfolio |
|---|---|---|---|
| 20 | | Property Value | 4,000,000 |
| | | Initial Debt | (700,000) |
| | W | Equity Used | (148,000) |
| | W | Less Holding Costs | (100,000) |
| | W | Less Equity Charge | (191,000) |
| | ? | **Total Remaining Equity** | **2,861,000** |

Paul and Sue have enjoyed another 10 years of equity growth without contributing any of their own money; in fact, their equity has more than doubled. Here's the summary of their position after 20 years, with just their home and one investment property.

| Years | Summary | | Total Portfolio |
|---|---|---|---|
| 20 | | Property Value | 4,000,000 |
| | | Initial Debt | (700,000) |
| | W | Equity Used | (439,000) |
| | ? | **Equity** | **2,861,000** |

We now move forward another 10 years, assuming again that the investment property still requires $10,000 a year to hold. Let's see their equity position after 30 years.

| Years | | Total Portfolio | |
|---|---|---|---|
| 30 | | Property Value | 8,000,000 |
| | | Initial Debt | (700,000) |
| | W | Equity Used | (439,000) |
| | W | Less Holding Costs | (100,000) |
| | W | Less Equity Charge | (472,000) |
| | ? | **Total Remaining Equity** | **6,289,000** |

Even with the $472,000 Equity Charge added in, Paul and Sue's equity has more than doubled once again.

| Years | Summary | | Total Portfolio |
|---|---|---|---|
| 30 | 🌏 | Property Value | 8,000,000 |
| | 🌏 | Initial Debt | (700,000) |
| | W | Equity Used | (1,011,000) |
| | ? | **Equity** | 6,289,000 |

Paul and Sue are now close to retirement age!

## Quick Recap

Just to make sure you're still with us, let's recap!

Paul and Sue, starting with $300,000 equity have, over a 30-year period, created a net worth of over six million dollars. This includes all debt and interest and this has required *none* of their own money. Of course, they could have used their own income to help fund a second investment property or more, but we'll leave those numbers to your imagination at this stage!

From here, we want to take you one step further and show you how it's possible to live off your equity.

# SECTION 3: LIVING OFF YOUR EQUITY

Let's go back in time and revisit Paul and Sue in their 20th investing year. You may recall that their position looked like this:

| Years | Summary | | Total Portfolio |
|---|---|---|---|
| 20 | 🌏 | Property Value | 4,000,000 |
| | 🌏 | Initial Debt | (700,000) |
| | W | Equity Used | (439,000) |
| | ? | **Equity** | **2,861,000** |

Keep in mind that this includes the cost of the investment property funding itself. We have already established that Paul and Sue can comfortably use their equity to self-fund their investment property; in other words, we know that they have enough of a time buffer to last each 10-year cycle.

Paul and Sue, after 20 years of investing, wonder if it's possible to start living off some of their equity. They'd like to earn an additional $100,000 per year and reduce their working hours so they can enjoy a bit of travel. Let's see if they can do it!

| **Equity Charge™ Calculator** | | | |
|---|---|---|---|
| Number of Years (Buying Time) | | 10 | years |
| Annual Holding Cost | $ | | |
| Annual Lifestyle Cost | $ | 100,000 | |
| Amount of Equity Already Used | $ | | |
| Annual Interest Rate | | 7.00% | |
| **Prediction for the next 10 years** | | | |
| Holding Costs | $ | - | |
| Lifestyle Costs | $ | 1,000,000 | |
| Equity Charge™ | $ | 478,360 | |
| Total Equity Required | $ | 1,478,360 | |

Using $100,000 of equity for the next 10 years adds up to $1,000,000 of equity. The Equity Charge on $1 million is approximately $480,000. That means they'll use $1.48 million over the next decade; and with an equity base of $2.861 million, this is achievable. However, we also need to incorporate the ongoing cost of their investment property. Here's how the numbers look using the Equity Charge Calculator.

| **Equity Charge™ Calculator** | | | |
|---|---|---|---|
| Number of Years (Buying Time) | | 10 | years |
| Annual Holding Cost | $ | 10,000 | |
| Annual Lifestyle Cost | $ | 100,000 | |
| Amount of Equity Already Used | $ | 439,000 | |
| Annual Interest Rate | | 7.00% | |
| **Prediction for the next 10 years** | | | |
| Holding Costs | $ | 100,000 | |
| Lifestyle Costs | $ | 1,000,000 | |
| Equity Charge™ | $ | 950,775 | |
| Total Equity Required | $ | 2,050,775 | |

Over the next decade, Paul and Sue have worked out that they might use up to $2.05 million worth of equity. This amount is set aside to self-fund their investment property and lifestyle. Using $2.05 million of their current $2.861 million leaves them with a buffer of $810,000.

Let's take a look at the picture at the end of that decade, in their 30th year of investing.

| Years | | | Total Portfolio |
|---|---|---|---|
| 30 | 🌏 | Property Value | 8,000,000 |
| | 🌏 | Initial Debt | (700,000) |
| | W | Equity Used | (439,000) |
| | W | Less Holding Costs | (100,000) |
| | ? | Less Lifestyle | (1,000,000) |
| | W | Less Equity Charge | (950,000) |
| | ? | **Total Remaining Equity** | **4,811,000** |

Paul and Sue now have $4.811 million in equity after 30 years, using none of their own money, and have received $100,000 tax-free for the last 10 years to help fund their lifestyle. While their debt has also risen, their asset base continues to increase at a rate faster than their spending. This is because they are doing it over *time* and are ensuring they have a buffer in place before they start using the money.

Hopefully, by now you can begin to see the power of using your equity and ensuring you have a big enough time buffer — enough equity to last 10 years.

If you are more aggressive, you might be happy with a buffer that lasts only seven years, or possibly less if you think the next wave is coming soon. Alternatively, you might want to factor in a buffer that lasts you 12 years, just to be sure. It doesn't matter what *you* consider *safe*, as long as you are comfortable; that's what is important. All you do is work out your holding costs, and the amount of time you want to buy, and adjust your Equity Charge accordingly.

Usually, clients continue to accumulate more than one property, checking their time buffer to make sure that they keep it safe. Some clients have come to us with millions of dollars worth of property and a few million in equity, but they are working really hard, earning an income to pay for it all. When we show them how it's possible to have their portfolio fund itself and for them to actually earn tax-free money, you can appreciate that they are elated, some to the point of tears.

There is an old adage of being "asset rich, but cash poor". This shows that if you're asset rich you can be cash rich too!

Impressive? Not really — it's just a matter of buying time!

## SUMMARY

We can't emphasise this enough — it needs to be safe. And safety comes from having access to your equity. This is best achieved through a line of credit. Once your credit facilities are in place, you can then plan your investing and ensure you can buy enough time for the market to do its job. As a Player, you need to review your position regularly and make sure you have enough of a buffer to last until the next property cycle.

One of the most critical aspects of the W4L strategy is obtaining finance and making sure it is structured correctly so that you can continue to access your equity. And that's the topic of the next chapter.

We hope you grasped the W4L strategy and realise that, in the end, wealth becomes a waiting game and it grows while you sleep!

# 10

# The Finance Game

One of the biggest stumbling blocks when following the *Wealth for Life* strategy is obtaining finance. Therefore, it's imperative that you understand how to best play the game of finance to your benefit.

One point to realise is how the banks view your assets and your debt. Let's take a look at your balance sheet from a bank's perspective.

## Your Balance Sheet

| **Assets** | | **Liabilities** | |
|---|---|---|---|
| Property | $500,000 | Loan | ($400,000) |

## Bank's Balance Sheet

| **Assets** | | Liabilities |
|---|---|---|
| Loan to you | $400,000 | |
| (secured by $500,000 property) | | |

The banks look at your loan as an asset, secured by property. The key factor for a bank is making it *safe* for *them*; therefore, they like to keep the value of the loan z **L**oan to **V**alue **R**atio (LVR) and is calculated as follows:

$$(\text{Loan/property value}) \times 100 = \text{LVR}\,\%$$

For example, putting some numbers into the formula above:

(Loan \$300,000/Property \$500,000) × 100 = 60%

Generally speaking, banks and lenders prefer to keep the LVR under 80%, which means they are prepared to lend only 80% of the asset value. The exception is when you first purchase a property; some lenders will lend more than 80% of the asset value, some even up to 100%.

## CROSS COLLATERALISATION

This is a special term that needs to be understood by the investor. *Collateral* is the security put up for a loan, such as a property. *Collateralisation* is the act of providing security for a loan. Cross collateralisation is the act of using lots of different assets as security for a single loan. In other words, the security for the loan *crosses* over and includes several assets; it's like a big blanket that covers everything.

Cross collateralisation is good for a bank, but bad for the investor.

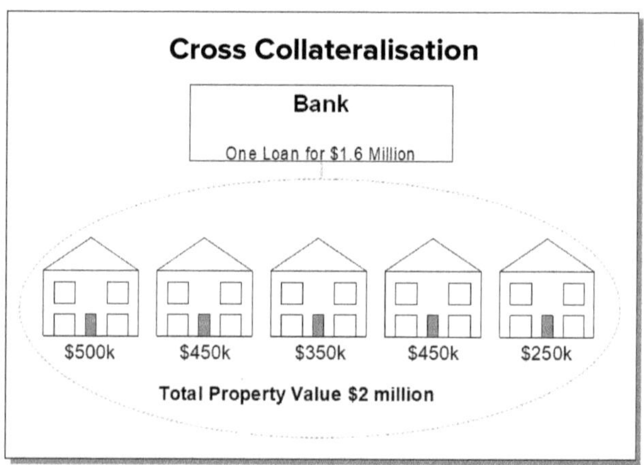


Your balance sheet would look like this:

## Your Balance Sheet — Cross Collateralisation

| Assets | | Liabilities | |
|---|---|---|---|
| Property 1 | $500,000 | Loan | ($1.6 million) |
| Property 2 | $450,000 | | |
| Property 3 | $350,000 | | |
| Property 4 | $450,000 | | |
| Property 5 | $250,000 | | |
| Total | $2 million | | |

In this example above, the LVR is 80%. Possible issues arise, however, when the bank has security over all your assets for a single loan. These issues are:

1. Restriction or an inability to borrow more money.

2. Defaulting on the loan puts *all* the properties at risk.

Let's discuss these issues in more detail.

The restriction to borrowing comes about because the bank assesses you and your assets as an individual risk. Once your asset value starts to be significant, to keep it safe for the bank, they reduce their LVR. On a million dollars worth of assets, they are happy to provide an 80% LVR ($800,000). But the more property you buy, the bigger your asset value. Having $5 million in assets at an 80% LVR is a $4 million loan. This might be getting too risky from the bank's perspective so they reduce their LVR to 70% or increase the interest rate. And if you understand the principles of leverage as contained in this book, all of a sudden you're being choked as an investor and are being prevented from playing the property investing game. Remember:

- **Debt is only a problem if you can't get more debt.**

The second issue is just as concerning. Should you, for whatever reason, suddenly have difficulty paying the loan, the bank can force the sale of the underlying assets. Because all properties are held as security, the lender could sell all the properties. These are called mortgagee sales; the lender with the mortgage over the property is the one selling. These are great news for the investor who is buying, but a sad tale for the investor who is forced to sell because such properties are often sold under market value. Why? Well, the lender normally has a loan of 80% of the property value (or less) and therefore is only really concerned with getting that 80% back. So if the property is sold for 90% of its value, the lender takes their share and the previous owner only receives 10% of the value of the property. It's often a fire sale[18] because the intention of the lender is to recoup the loan amount, not to try to make a profit.

The solution for the two issues above is to keep your property loans separate; try not to cross collateralise. This means you would have a different loan for each property.

## Your Balance Sheet

| Assets | | Liabilities | |
|---|---|---|---|
| Property 1 | $500,000 | Loan 1 | ($400,000) |
| Property 2 | $450,000 | Loan 2 | ($360,000) |
| Property 3 | $350,000 | Loan 3 | ($280,000) |
| Property 4 | $450,000 | Loan 4 | ($360,000) |
| Property 5 | $250,000 | Loan 5 | ($200,000) |
| Total | $2 million | Total | ($1.6 million) |

This is more effort on your part and it requires more paperwork, but to avoid being choked as an investor it is necessary. By having separate loans you maintain control. In the case of defaulting, it might be possible to refinance a single property and get yourself temporarily out of trouble. On the other hand, you simply might not be able to afford a particular property so you're forced to sell that one property in a fire sale but the rest remain secure.

18 **fire sale:** sale of assets at very low prices, typically when the seller faces bankruptcy.

## USING DIFFERENT BANKS

Organising separate loans, as described above, often requires that you use separate banks or lenders. If negotiation with your current lender fails to come to the agreement of keeping all assets separate, then the only alternative is to refinance your existing assets with your current bank by obtaining a line of credit. You then use some of that line of credit as a deposit on the new property and finance it with a different lender.

By following this method, you turned a liability into an asset immediately (from the new lender's point of view). This diagram explains what we mean:

### Your Balance Sheet with Lender #1

| **Assets** | | **Liabilities** | |
|---|---|---|---|
| Property | $500,000 | Loan | ($300,000) |
| | | Deposit on new property | ($100,000) |

**Your Balance Sheet from the New Lender's View**

| **Assets** | | **Liabilities** | |
|---|---|---|---|
| Property | $500,000 | Loan (with lender #1) | ($400,000) |
| Cash | $100,000 | | |

When you approach another lender, they look at your $100,000 draw down of cash as an asset. This makes them more willing to lend, as your balance sheets look strong. This is one way to keep your loans separate.

## THE VALUATION GAME

All banks and lenders have several valuation companies that they use to value property. The banks don't value property; it must be done by a qualified valuer.

When purchasing a property or refinancing an existing one, a valuer is required to present a written valuation of the property. The bank lends against this valuation.

The Player following the W4L strategy knows that accessing more finance provides a bigger buffer and buys more time. A Player also understands the vital role a valuer plays in this game.

When refinancing properties, the banks will only provide you with 80% of the total value. Imagine if you had three different valuers provide you with the following valuations:

Valuer 1: $450,000

Valuer 2: $500,000

Valuer 3: $550,000

The difference between valuer 1 and valuer 3 is $100,000, which can mean seven to eight years of additional time for the investor in which this property could be self-funding. But why would the valuers provide different valuations? A property valuation is a matter of opinion. A valuer makes a judgment based on facts such as recent sales, type of property, the area and so on. Your job as a Player is to convince a valuer of the value of your property with facts to support your opinion.

This truly is a game! First, you find out which companies are on the panel of valuers that your lender uses. Then call them up and invite them to value your property. (This does cost you money, by the way; a valuation for residential property ranges from $400 to $2500.) When you meet with the valuer it's your job to show them why the property is worth $X. Provide them with recent sales information in the area, point out improvements you've made to the property, explain about new infrastructure such as roads, schools, etc. Provide them with all the reasons to prove the property is worth $X.

You'll be amazed at what a difference this can make to a valuation. And every dollar extra buys you more time. If the valuer disagrees with your estimates or falls too short, that's okay; just call in another one.

A fantastic example of this is a real life story from a client of ours. They wanted to revalue their investment property to increase their buffer. The tenant living in the premises had clean, yet old, furniture that made the place look a little shabby. So they put the tenant up in a hotel for a couple of days (to the tenant's delight!); then they removed all the old furniture and replaced it with new, more stylish furniture. They gave the place a good clean, a bit of paint, added some flowers and made it really homey. When the valuer came, he saw a beautiful, well-kept home and over a nice cup of tea was shown all the recent sales in the area.

The valuation came in at $180,000 more than the last valuation. And no sooner had the valuer left than the removalist truck returned to move all the new furniture out and the old stuff back in.

Our clients had *created* enough equity to self-fund the property for about 10 years. Or they could use it as a deposit on another property. And consider this — that $180,000 is totally tax free.

You see, it truly is a game that can be fun!

## CREATE YOUR TIME BUFFER BEFORE PLAYING THE GAME

This method can also be applied to buying. Before you purchase a property, outline your planned improvements to the valuer: a new kitchen, a new bathroom, some paint, landscaping etc. Show the valuer what you plan to do and get their opinion on what they think it will be worth. And get them to put it in writing. If you do it in this sequence it means that you can buy the property knowing that if you do those improvements, the buffer is there to take care of itself.

One client of ours was interested in buying a property for $2.4 million in Mosman, NSW, but before buying the property, he called three different valuers and asked them how they would value the property if he was to make several improvements. The first two would base their valuation on the purchase price only, plus the cost of improvements. The third, however, indicated it could be worth $3.2 million after the renovations. Armed with this information, the client worked out his holding strategy *before* he purchased.

He purchased the property and spent $130,000 on renovations. The valuer was called back and the property was revalued at $3.2 million. The total cost to the client was $2.65 million (including stamp duty and renovation costs). Therefore, the immediate profit was $550,000. Of course, this client knows not to sell; instead, he refinanced the property and obtained a line of credit. The holding cost on this property was approximately $90,000 per year, which meant he had bought about four to five years in time. More recently, this property was re-valued at $3.6 million.

It is much easier to get a property re-valued at $3.2 million than it is to sell it for that much. And if it was sold, the cost of agent's fees and capital gains tax immediately reduces the profits. Our philosophy is to keep the profits *and* the asset so that you can continue to enjoy and use the capital growth.

## GETTING YOUR BUFFER IN PLACE

Having your finances in place is the key to ensuring you have bought enough time to last until the next property cycle. Whenever a property value has improved, it is worthwhile to increase the line of credit on that property. The *cost* of refinancing should be looked upon as an *investment* to access more equity. This viewpoint is entirely different to the norm. If it costs you $5000 in fees to exit one loan but that now means you have access to an extra $100,000, you have in effect generated an extra $95,000, which may help fund a property for several years.

This is how the Player also views mortgage insurance, the cost of which allows you to access an extra 10% to 15% of the equity. Next time you have the opportunity, do your numbers and see how much extra time you can buy using mortgage insurance.

Understanding these principles and knowing the value of having access to equity, the Player needs to keep their eye on the property market and, at the very least, refinance at the peak of each cycle, as illustrated below.

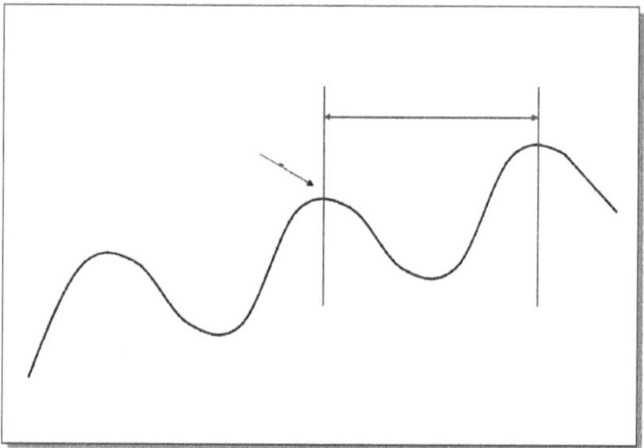

By doing this, the Player has established their time buffer for the coming years. After the boom is over and prices have settled down, the Player (ready with available funds) goes on a buying spree building up their asset base, knowing that it's the size of their assets that matters!

# PART 3:
# Inspiring Real-Life Stories

# 11

# Inspiring Real Life Stories

It is truly an honour to be able to share these wonderful stories with you. All of the people you're about to meet have either made it or are well on their way to success. Each has had their struggle one way or another. We hope that by sharing these stories you will see that it can be done by anyone. There are definitely some key ingredients to being a successful investor, but they are not charisma, charm or luck! You'll discover — as you read through these stories — that success comes through taking action and believing in yourself.

We have left a few lines at the end of each story for you to note down what you learned from it. These notes can become your signposts that motivate you and keep you on track as you continue on your road to wealth.

If you are new to investing or are just starting out, we hope that by reading these stories, you might recognise some similarities with your own situation and are given enough inspiration to do something about it.

If you're an experienced investor with a solid asset base, we hope that you are inspired to do more and move to an even greater position of strength.

And whether young or old, experienced or a novice, we hope that you are inspired to build real wealth for life, for yourself, your family and society.

Enjoy!

**Please note:** The opinions of the contributors to this section are not to be taken as advice for your own situation. As with all information in this book, readers need to seek their own independent advice from the appropriately qualified people.

# Shane and Melissa

"I finished high school at age 17 and started an apprenticeship as a fitter and turner. Knowing I was on very good money for a young fella, I saved up a deposit and, at age 19, bought my first house."

## Portfolio Snapshot

| **Name** | Shane |
|---|---|
| **Portfolio** | 4 properties |
| **Approximate Value** | $960,000 |
| **Total Debt** | $860,000 |
| **Net Worth (Equity)** | $100,000 |
| **Current Income** | $68,000 |

## What made you get into property investing?

My best friend's father is a real estate agent so from a young age I have watched him grow his wealth from property and when I started full-time work he wanted me to do the same.

## What mistakes have you made?

Renting to family would have to be my biggest mistake.

## What is the biggest lesson you could pass on?

Knowledge is power, so learn all you can and know that there is a lot of noise out there about property investing; sort through it and find what's right for you.

## Tell us about your life before you were an investor ...

Not much to tell. I was a teenage boy into cars, sports and chasing girls for most of it, just before getting an apprenticeship. Then I started investing.

## Tell us your story of how it all started ...

I finished high school at age 17 and started an apprenticeship as a fitter and turner. Knowing I was on very good money for a young fella, I saved up a deposit and, at age 19, I bought my first house. After some mentoring from my mate's father, I used the First Home Owners Grant from the government and some of my own money to buy my second at age 20. The rest is history, as they say!

## What is life like, now that you are an investor?

Scary at times, as I feel that I am doing something wrong because no one my age (I'm 26 now) has done what I have, that I know of anyway. But at the same time, life is good, knowing that my future is looking bright. I see all the old guys at work putting as much money as they can into superannuation because they did not invest when they were young. I'm glad I don't have to worry like that.

## What is your reason for doing this? Why are you an investor?

I look at investing in property as not buying houses, but buying *time* to do the things that I want to do in life. That is why I invest.

### Has anyone ever told you to "be careful" or "play it safe"? If so, how did you handle it?

Yes, my family told me that many times and it made me scared, but then after talking to my best friend's father, who is like my mentor, I realised that if I wanted to be like my family then listen to them, but if I wanted more than that I needed to believe in myself.

### Were you or are you ever discouraged by others? If so, what happened?

I have heard some stories of people not doing well in property but found, when I heard more of their story, they had little or no knowledge and that's where they went wrong.

### What words of encouragement would you give to an investor who is starting out?

Believe in yourself and obtain the knowledge needed to be successful. Listen to people who are in the position you want to be in.

### What do you think about the Wealth for Life strategy?

I think it's great. Anything that helps people become self-funded in retirement and not rely on the government for help is great. I'm all for it — keep up the good work, guys!

### Is there anything else you'd like to say?

I would just like to say to anyone thinking of investing in property, "Do it!" Don't sit on the fence thinking, as there's no better time than today to start and you won't regret it!

* * *

***What did you get from reading this story?***

# Luca

"Over the last 12 years I have been able to travel, including 12 months backpacking around Europe, the UK and Ireland; two months in Greece and Turkey; numerous trips to Fiji, Bali, New Zealand and within Australia. All using my equity, while my assets are still maintaining great growth."

## Portfolio Snapshot

| Name | Luca |
|---|---|
| Portfolio | 3 properties |
| Approximate Value | $1.05 million |
| Total Debt | $840,000 |
| Net Worth (Equity) | $210,000 |
| Current Income | Currently nil — starting a new business |

## What made you get into property investing?

To facilitate more freedom. Financial freedom equals freedom of choice, of lifestyle. I believe property is the easiest and most secure way to manufacture wealth.

## What mistakes have you made?

My first two properties — one in Narellan Vale, NSW, and one in Research, Victoria — were purchased to live in, not as investments. They are examples of where not to buy, yet they have achieved great capital growth.

My biggest mistake was having the traditional mindset and taking 10 years to pay the first one off before I purchased the second, then a further six years to purchase the third. The next mistake was purchasing the second property in two names rather than my own, even though my then partner contributed nothing, except for his income statement for the loan. I now know that I could have done it by myself.

## What is the biggest lesson you could pass on?

To start as early as you can and purchase the next property as soon as you have sufficient equity to put down a deposit and enough cashflow to cover expenses while the properties continue to grow. Also, borrow as much as you can when you can, to cover the normal property cycle and any rainy days, or to keep you cashed up if you decide to start a business.

I purchased my first property shortly after I turned 22. I remember thinking that $110,000 would take a lifetime of sacrifice to pay off but I didn't care because I had built a house and it was mine.

## Tell us about your life before you were an investor ...

Life was financially insecure. As a single woman, if I wasn't working, I wasn't earning an income. There was never enough money or time to do anything other than work and pay the mortgage. That's not my idea of fun. The novelty of owning a home wears thin when all you experience is within those same walls. I eventually found out there was a much better way to both live and own property.

## Tell us your story of how it all started ...

Coming from a good Italian background, I purchased my first property in 1990 at age 22. I then proceeded to work and pay this property off over the next 10 years. Luckily, I then moved interstate to South Australia for two years, renting it out, and then I moved to Melbourne for a further six years. When I arrived in Melbourne, planning to stay for a while, I used the equity in the first home to purchase a second. I continued to work and pay off both mortgages with a limiting belief that I was maxed out on borrowing capacity and cashflow. I then changed my mindset and decided to become a property investor and business owner. I then moved back to my Sydney home, rented out the Research property, borrowed more and purchased a perfect two-bedroom unit in Elwood, Victoria. My new business will soon be generating income and I will continue to purchase properties more aggressively, using options such as joint ventures and vendor finance.

## What is life like, now that you are an investor?

It's fabulous. Currently I have had the last 12 months off while moving back to Sydney to become an investor and business owner. I have been able to spend time and money on increasing my knowledge in both personal development and mindset, which is critical, plus in all areas of property knowledge.

Two years ago, I also had six months off while changing careers again from IT to Event Management, trying to find my passion. I soon realised that I could combine my passion for property and helping others as a successful business career.

Over the last 12 years I have been able to travel, including 12 months backpacking around Europe and the UK; two months in Greece and Turkey; numerous trips to Fiji, Bali, New Zealand and within Australia. All using my equity, while my assets are still maintaining great growth.

## What is your reason for doing this? Why are you an investor?

The same reason I got into it, which was to give me more freedom. To me, financial freedom is about freedom of choice and of lifestyle. Property is the easiest and most secure way to manufacture wealth. Now I've turned my passion into a business empowering other single women to become successful property investors.

### Has anyone ever told you to “be careful” or “play it safe”? If so, how did you handle it?

Yes, everyone. You just realise that whatever 97% of the population say and do, you do the opposite. You associate yourself with other successful investors and create a mastermind group who can guide and support you with advice and ideas from their own experiences.

### Were you or are you ever discouraged by others? If so, what happened?

Not now that I am a true property investor. I only listen to and take advice from people with more properties than myself, not those with one or none. You just need to understand that the majority of the population have the wrong mindset for investing which is why I have created my business to help change that.

### What words of encouragement would you give to an investor who is starting out?

That anyone can become an investor as long as you are committed long term and have the right mindset and education regarding finances and the property market. I also encourage people to use the services of like-minded business people and to employ experts in each field, all the while remaining in charge of their property business.

### What do you think about the Wealth for Life strategy?

I love the Wealth for Life strategy. I live the Wealth for Life strategy. It truly amazes me that with such a simple strategy of purchasing one property, then forever using your equity to buy the next property, that more people are not doing so. I recommend that single women start now and get their foot in the door of the property market as soon as possible. Sacrifice some luxuries and instant gratification now, with the knowledge of greater wealth and freedom a little further down the track.

## Is there anything else you'd like to say?

Yes, that as scary as it may seem as a single woman to get into considerable "good" debt to buy property, it is much scarier if you don't and remain financially insecure. Life is too short to trade working hours for money.

Single women have to empower themselves in the traditionally male areas of finance and investing. They will then realise they do not need to be part of a couple to purchase their first property and go on and become successful property investors. Women are strong, smart and business savvy and have all the resources they need within themselves to get into the market and become wealthy investors.

* * *

***What did you get from reading this story?***

# Sara

"I was in a marriage with a melancholy, phlegmatic man who analysed yet did nothing. I got frustrated with not being allowed to invest so I got divorced and bought property!"

## Portfolio Snapshot

| **Name** | Sara |
|---|---|
| **Portfolio** | 2 properties |
| **Approximate Value** | $425,000 |
| **Total Debt** | $210,000 |
| **Net Worth (Equity)** | $215,000 |
| **Current Income** | $23,473 |

### What made you get into property investing?

I understand that property increases in value at a higher rate than anything else.

### What mistakes have you made?

I have allowed others to make decisions for me. I bought a property that was one of 23 in an estate with all the surrounding houses being units and townhouses. I then sold the property for $250K and bought a new house but I should not have sold. Over the next four years, the original townhouse grew in value by 80% whereas the new house only grew by 25%! There were no other developments in the area to get a valuation on the new house.

### What is the biggest lesson you could pass on?

Read lots of personal development books and surround yourself with the people you want to be like.

### Tell us about your life before you were an investor ...

Life's always been good; however, now I am in control of creating my life to become who I want to be.

### Tell us your story of how it all started ...

I was in a marriage with a melancholy, phlegmatic man who analysed yet did nothing. I got frustrated with not being allowed to invest so I got divorced and bought property!

### What is life like now that you are an investor?

Interesting! I now have the ability to do what I want, when I want and from now on will leverage, leverage, leverage.

### What is your reason for doing this? Why are you an investor?

I realised that I spent too much money and always needed more. Whenever I have focused on manifesting an increase in money, property has always come up.

**Has anyone ever told you to "be careful" or "play it safe"? If so, how did you handle it?**

I laugh, since the only time I succeed is when I live "dangerously". I also have more fun in life when I am doing the opposite to the status quo.

**Were you or are you ever discouraged by others? If so, what happened?**

No, I believe what doesn't kill you makes you stronger.

**What words of encouragement would you give to an investor who is starting out?**

Set your goal and just do it. Read, read, read and enjoy the journey.

**What do you think about the Wealth for Life strategy?**

It's great to finally have a team to work with who are passionate about helping others.

**Is there anything else you'd like to say?**

The buck stops here. We are all where we are now through choices we have made. If you are not happy with where you are right now, make a different decision.

* * *

*What did you get from reading this story?*

# Eddie

"The first property purchase is usually the most difficult and is filled with doubt. In fact, my first property purchase has achieved the most capital gain of them all."

## Portfolio Snapshot

| **Name** | Eddie |
|---|---|
| **Portfolio** | 4 properties |
| **Approximate Value** | $700,000 |
| **Total Debt** | $440,000 |
| **Net Worth (Equity)** | $260,000 |

## What made you get into property investing?

I wanted to have a situation of being financially independent, which meant only working if I really wanted to.

## What mistakes have you made?

Not doing enough research on one of the properties. This is the key for getting enough equity to purchase another property.

## What is the biggest lesson you could pass on?

To be absolutely sure that you will get capital growth in the property that is chosen. Also to be aware of what stage of the property cycle you are investing in — that is, the boom or the bust.

## Tell us about your life before you were an investor ...

I was working in my own company contracting, trading time for money. I had the mindset of, "The more time I put in, the more money I get," which I now know is not entirely true.

## Tell us your story of how it all started ...

Actually it all started when a friend of mine went to a property course held in Sydney and this person showed me how it's possible to create a living through property investing. I really didn't believe him that much until *another* friend showed me how he was able to keep building property as his principal place of residence and live on it by selling up after two years and building another even bigger one. He was basically living on his equity. I then started reading different books on the subject and that made me decide to start investing in property.

## What is life like now that you are an investor?

Well, I haven't really achieved my goal of not needing to work yet but every year I get a nice cheque back from the government which I wouldn't have if I didn't invest in property.

**What is your reason for doing this? Why are you an investor?**

Freedom to do whatever I want, whenever I want. Currently I still have to work as a means to an end and I don't think life should be like that.

**Has anyone ever told you to "be careful" or "play it safe"? If so, how did you handle it?**

Yes, my mum, who is always concerned about my welfare. But I think she is too cautious and doesn't understand the full picture. I just tell her that I have gone to enough courses and I know what I am doing.

**Were you or are you ever discouraged by others? If so, what happened?**

Sometimes, but I think that having known two people who are also succeeding as property investors gives me an incentive. My other friends who don't invest are basically a bit too scared to try it. It's kind of a Catch 22 situation; they don't know so they don't try.

**What words of encouragement would you give to an investor who is starting out?**

I definitely recommend you do a few courses and, if you can, ask questions from people who are doing property investments especially if they are a close friend. The first property purchase is usually the most difficult and is filled with doubt. In fact, my first property purchase has achieved the most capital gain of them all.

**What do you think about the Wealth for Life strategy?**

I have read a few similar ideas and this solidifies that this strategy works.

**Is there anything else you'd like to say?**

It's great to have qualified accountants who understand property and help look after my portfolio.

* * *

***What did you get from reading this story?***

# Garry

"A side effect of property investing is that it does wonders for character building as well as developing those decision muscles!"

## Portfolio Snapshot

| **Name** | Garry |
|---|---|
| **Portfolio** | 8 properties |
| **Approximate Value** | $3.7 million |
| **Total Debt** | $3.4 million |
| **Net Worth (Equity)** | $300,000 |
| **Current Income** | Me $65k; my wife $35k |

### What made you get into property investing?

I believe that superannuation is not the answer and wealth is achieved through property investing.

### What mistakes have you made?

I made too many assumptions without investigating. Also, I used only one lender. Early on, my focus was short-term rather than long-term planning.

### What is the biggest lesson you could pass on?

Do not do the loans yourself; find a good broker. Do not be swayed by what the masses tell you are good areas to invest in and be prepared to learn.

### Tell us about your life before you were an investor ...

Caretaker. Still am!

### Tell us your story of how it all started ...

I came from the country, my wife from China. I had small-town thinking, in that for $300k I could buy acres in the country rather than a one-bedroom unit in Sydney. We do not have our own home. We just about killed each other to get that 10% deposit.

From the first property purchase, I became a sponge for information on property investing. I went to all the free seminars I could and read. I took all the information in at face value, but I had to take responsibility for my decisions. I doubted everything that was said until I could prove it was true.

We decided after 12 months to look at a second property. We looked at Defence Housing Australia for properties (these are properties rented out by the government for Australian Defence personnel). We went to Canberra to check out their catalogue of properties but took a wrong turn and came across a group of townhouses being built. I asked about them and found that they were all sold. I thought, "Now that's interesting." The only other place I had seen that happen was in the sought-after beach suburb of Manly, NSW. So we started investing in Canberra and haven't left. We've even stuck with the same agent and building company with our investments.

### What is life like, now that you are an investor?

Very tight, as this year we have purchased six and sold one. But this is the basis for our future wealth so we'll keep on going.

### What is your reason for doing this? Why are you an investor?

We consider it our retirement fund.

### Has anyone ever told you to "be careful" or "play it safe"? If so, how did you handle it?

This has happened. I will listen, and try and find out why they are saying it. It is most likely to be:

1. They have not been successful.

2. Tall poppy syndrome.

3. You are moving up and they are stagnating.

4. They are trapped within their perceived boundaries by their thinking.

### Were you or are you ever discouraged by others? If so, what happened?

Never!

### What words of encouragement would you give to an investor who is starting out?

Any property investing carries a certain amount of risk. But if you do your own research, you can reduce it. Be prepared to look at 10 years down the track. Act on your convictions!

### What do you think about the Wealth for Life strategy?

It sounds good. People first need the confidence. It has nothing to do with income or where you live.

### Is there anything else you'd like to say?

A side effect of property investing is that it does wonders for character building as well as developing those decision muscles!

* * *

***What did you get from reading this story?***

# Cherie

"I realised, belatedly, that a good salary will not get one there, so at 63 I am still forging ahead, albeit slowly and cautiously, only buying the best property in the best location I can afford."

## Portfolio Snapshot

| **Name** | Cherie |
|---|---|
| **Portfolio** | 3 properties |
| **Approximate Value** | $1.1 million |
| **Total Debt** | $330,000 |
| **Net Worth (Equity)** | $770,000 |
| **Current Income** | $29,000 Super pension<br>$30,000 rental income<br>Working part-time as well |

## What made you get into property investing?

I could make sense of the system once I had read enough books. I am also fiercely protective of my own three wonderful adult children and six beautiful grandchildren so I want to be able to leave something to them and secure a future for my husband and myself at the same time. That is what drives me. I was also on my own from the age of 18 and realised, "If it is to be, it is up to me" — the 10 most powerful two-letter words in the English language! I realised, belatedly, that a good salary will not get one there, so at 63 I am still forging ahead, albeit slowly and cautiously, only buying the best property in the best location I can afford.

## What mistakes have you made?

Selling my houses. Big mistake! I used to trade houses — buy and then do it up while living there, sell and move on to the next one. What I did not know or understand was the system of "buy and hold". If only! I guess we all have those stories.

The trick is to just keep moving forward as we only have the here and now with the future only a possibility; the past has gone, a spent cheque. Despite my age, time is still a best friend. The point is, time is passing us by anyhow, so I figure one may as well stay with the system. Retirement, in that sense, is not for me.

## What is the biggest lesson you could pass on?

The best lesson I could pass on is to be vigilant; to grab hold of life and not let life pass one by. To ensure one treats others as one would like to be treated; that is, with consideration, respect, caring, compassion and understanding: Good old-fashioned manners actually. Money is really only the vehicle to becoming a better person, more able to contribute to our families, community and society in a positive way.

## Tell us about your life before you were an investor ...

As a little girl I always loved playing cubbyhouses, which included making dirt floor plans, tree houses and cubbyhouses down in the back garden. So it probably developed from there.

I built a beautiful Gabriel Poole-designed house with my first husband on the edges of the Blackall Ranges overlooking the Glasshouse Mountains, Queensland. A credit squeeze hit back in 1974 and, combined with a rural recession, property prices tumbled by half — real boom and bust stuff. No one back then was able to say to me, "If you don't sell, you don't lose." I wish they had!

On relocating from Queensland to Tasmania at that time, I realised I personally needed a qualification if I was to be economically viable in my own right. A Social Science degree followed and employment for 25 years in a variety of Commonwealth Departments as a public servant who did up houses on the side. Three wonderful adult children, six equally beautiful grandchildren and a wonderful farmer husband now complete me!

It is really only in the last few years that I have had the time to read and educate myself as to how *real* money is made, hence my continuing journey.

### Tell us your story of how it all started ...

It started as a little girl with an avid interest in property. I bumbled along for so many years without the right advice and continued to trade my own homes by doing them up and selling them for a modest profit. I did this a total of, wait for it, nine times before considering there was another way. That is, buy and hold, buy and hold, buy and hold, ad infinitum!

Not until about 2003 did the penny finally drop, even though I had read the books. Some of us are just slow learners, I guess! I did keep one house, bought in 1995 for $85,000 and now worth $285,000 and another waterfront property, bought in 2001 for $135,000 now worth $500,000. You see, it was not until the definitive works of yourselves and others, did it finally all make sense. My story is only a small-time one, but one CAN begin the journey and never, ever stop remembering to always *enjoy* the journey.

### What is life like, now that you are an investor?

Always interesting and I meet so many good people along the way. Life is very busy yet doing up a house over the phone and with internet pictures is a challenge unless one has great people around, including good tradesmen, which I do. I certainly do not have time for renovating it myself but I do enjoy the creative, visual process of turning "sow's ears into silk purses", so to speak. I love the worst house in the best street.

## What is your reason for doing this, why are you an investor?

I have a burning ambition to provide for my family, perhaps because my own family did precisely the opposite for me. I am also acutely aware of the old adage "Don't feed them fish but teach them to fish" which is what I do. I HOPE to provide them with a role model as well as the books and DVDs on the subject of property acquisition as an investment tool to help them internalise the concepts I so belatedly learned.

## Has anyone ever told you to "be careful" or "play it safe"? If so, how did you handle it?

Most of my friends think I am mad. I just say, "It's okay, I would find it less safe if I did not take action." And at least with "bricks and mortar" it still sits there even if there is a downturn, unlike shares which could leave one with a big fat zero on paper. I find there is jealousy and envy out there too, even with the very modest portfolio I have accumulated.

## Were you or are you ever discouraged by others? If so, what happened?

I sold two units in Cairns, North Queensland, as I believed it was lacking the job infrastructure there for sustained growth, being heavily dependent on tourism and builders. I believed builders kept on building units just to keep their cashflow happening and to avoid the bankruptcy wave engulfing them. However, in hindsight, the units were well positioned near major shopping outlets and would have slowly crept up in value, even if just because of the rise in building materials and wages. I have belatedly learned to never, never sell — ever!

## What words of encouragement would you give to an investor who is starting out?

Just keep on keeping on. Do not be deterred by others. Many people would prefer to see one reduced to the lowest common denominator, I'm afraid. They are sometimes the ones driving the big cars, yet not even owning the hub caps. Remember that the most successful people do not have to look rich to prove themselves.

### What do you think about the Wealth for Life strategy?

Excellent! I do need to learn more about the Wealth for Life strategy. That is about how to use the equity to fund lifestyle. Currently I have returned to part-time work, but know there is a better way to free up time. That is what is important to me; my personal needs are not lavish. I live with my husband on a broadacre farming property.

### Is there anything else you'd like to say?

Just that, "If it is to be it is up to me," and we DO have choices in life up to a point, other than say major health drawbacks. It is important to get over the belief that wealthy people are inherently less good, which is a quite prevalent, insidious belief I have found. Such a belief is a big mistake with very faulty thinking. The old adage that "one doesn't need money to be happy" is the biggest con there is. As one property investor said, "If you don't like being rich you can always go back to being poor!"

* * *

***What did you get from reading this story?***

# Melissa, Chris and family

"We are both fairly risk-averse and had to be absolutely sure that we could do it. With two small children in the picture as well, we could not afford costly mistakes."

## Portfolio Snapshot

| **Name** | Melissa and Chris |
|---|---|
| **Portfolio** | 3 properties |
| **Approximate Value** | $1.5 million |
| **Total Debt** | $1.1 million |
| **Net Worth (Equity)** | $400,000 |
| **Current Income** | $105,000 |

## What made you get into property investing?

We attended several workshops and seminars, read some books and spent many nights crunching numbers to satisfy ourselves that we could do this. We are both fairly risk adverse and had to be absolutely sure that we could do it. With two small children in the picture as well, we could not afford costly mistakes.

## What mistakes have you made?

We sold one! Before we caught on to the "buy and hold" and "use your equity" strategies, we sold our own home in 2004. We had purchased it in 2001 and it had appreciated from $485,000 to $650,000. If we had known what we do now, we would have used the equity instead of selling.

## What is the biggest lesson you could pass on?

Get as much knowledge as you can. In this way, while you can still be cautious and risk-moderate, you do not have to fear large mortgages and can begin to change the way you think about debt.

## Tell us about your life before you were an investor ...

We were, as our parents raised us, thinking that "debt is bad", and "you need to pay off your house as soon as you can".

## Tell us your story of how it all started ...

We "fell into it" to start with when my partner purchased a property that his parents lived in. When they moved, we all of a sudden had an investment property to deal with. Then, after attending several workshops and seminars, we decided it was an achievable course of action to wealth creation and worked towards our next investment.

## What is life like, now that you are an investor?

It's a mixed bag. We are on what we hope is the tail end of the slump in Sydney and are seeing all sorts of possible investments that we cannot afford to finance at the moment, so that is frustrating. However, we are patient and will bide our time until we can invest again.

**What is your reason for doing this? Why are you an investor?**

Our initial reason was to be self-funded retirees. I don't think that has changed, although maybe our goal posts are lifting.

**Has anyone ever told you to "be careful" or "play it safe"? If so, how did you handle it?**

We told them that we are being careful and we are playing it safe. Properly investing in property should be a boring, safe, long-term venture and so it is with us. We have done the sums and feel comfortable with the results. We have used our equity along with loans to buy time and so we have put aside money in the form of a line of credit loan that we can draw down over the next 10 years to cover any shortfalls that we may have.

**Were you or are you ever discouraged by others? If so, what happened?**

No. We were careful in our research and are comfortable with our decisions.

**What words of encouragement would you give to an investor who is starting out?**

It can be done! My youngest brother is busily saving his deposit to launch into the market and we are rallying behind him to help him achieve the same dream.

**What do you think about the Wealth for Life strategy?**

With careful planning and research, most people can achieve it. We should try very hard to be independent in our wealth.

**Is there anything else you'd like to say?**

Our most recent investment (August 2006) was purchased through a trust structure. We will do this again.

* * *

***What did you get from reading this story?***

# Jojo, Shona and family

"During the months that the property was under contract we decided to study more about property and the processes that developers use. We hit just about every property website and started to attend property seminars. We came to realise that we were sitting on gold, so during the contract period and with the help of our parents, we bought our second at an auction."

## Portfolio Snapshot

| | |
|---|---|
| **Name** | Jojo |
| **Portfolio** | 4½ properties |
| **Approximate Value** | $1.7 million |
| **Total Debt** | $1.25 million |
| **Net Worth (Equity)** | $450,000 |
| **Current Income** | $19,000 |

### What made you get into property investing?

Desperation! Financial desperation — and, more importantly, it was desperation to find our own niche in this world. My brothers and their partners were successful in their own right and here we were, still living day to day, struggling to find direction with our lives.

### What mistakes have you made?

No mistakes, just lessons we have taught ourselves. I have found that everyone is on a journey and no one is 100% certain about theirs. Even the experts are still learning, only they are at a different stage. For me, it comes down to accountability. Knowing and living this takes some work but the rewards are immeasurable. Also, gratitude is important; to have this is special and divine.

### What is the biggest lesson you could pass on?

Keep learning and sharing.

### Tell us about your life before you were an investor ...

I was a student with a family so we were quite poor and I was looking for a way to get our break.

### Tell us your story of how it all started ...

We bought a two-and-a-quarter acre block in 2001; this was our first house. We managed to sell it under a six-month developer's contract in 2004. We thought all our Christmas wishes had come true, but the contract didn't come to fruition and we didn't get the sale.

During the months that the property was under contract we decided to study more about property and the processes that developers use. We hit just about every property website and started to attend property seminars. We came to realise that we were sitting on gold so during the contract period, and with the help of our parents, we bought our second at an auction. We renovated this over a year; it was during this stage we were becoming more aware of creating equity through renovating.

In 2005 we refinanced our first property; late 2005 we refinanced our second; in mid-2006 we refinanced and got our third; early 2007 we refinanced for our fourth; and now we are about to refinance to get our fifth in partnership with a friend. And all the while we are learning and understanding that there is a lot more to learn!

### What is life like, now that you are an investor?

We are able to do a lot more with a lot less worry. And best of all we share what we have learned from you and others with our friends and family.

### What is your reason for doing this? Why are you an investor?

To give us the lifestyle we want, although we're not there yet, but we are on our way!

### Has anyone ever told you to "be careful" or "play it safe"? If so, how did you handle it?

No, actually no one has. Probably because they know how strong-willed we are. We haven't waited around for anyone to tell us to take it easy or be careful. Come to think of it, we started this journey with no other choice; we kept being told that we did not have enough experience to get the job, were too qualified for the position.

I had been studying Bachelor of Health Science (Naturopathy). When I sent out my CVs for positions, more often than not the response was I did not have enough experience, and then when I went for part-time manual work to supplement our income while studying, I was told that I was overqualified. Even when I was successful in getting the job, there was no inspiration or motivation from within to build a career out of it.

I can still remember the final days working part-time at a local factory. We had to get up at 4 a.m. to start work at 5 a.m. and I remember how inconvenient it was because Shona had to wake up as well (with the baby) to drop me off at the factory. We will never forget that special moment when Shona and I decided that there was more to life than this.

We decided to change our lives. I quit my job and we embarked on this property investing journey. The rest is history. Since then we have had to do the hard yards, we had to make the hard decisions, we had to sacrifice our weekends and spare time, but this time we were doing it for ourselves. We realised, and are still realising, that to become successful we had to inspire ourselves and we had to be accountable.

### Were you or are you ever discouraged by others? If so, what happened?

Yes, but momentarily. Usually we surround ourselves with positive material and knowledge in the form of DVDs, audios CDs and self-help information.

### What words of encouragement would you give to an investor who is starting out?

You can do it! Don't buy into everyone's "do's and don'ts". Create your own.

### What do you think about the Wealth for Life strategy?

The series was good to have on DVDs so I could relearn and clarify the principles and share them with my family and friends.

* * *

***What did you get from reading this story?***

# Alice

"My first job was working in the mines, where I met a lot of older people who have worked there for years and made a lot of money but have nothing to show for it. I realised then and there that I don't want to be like them, so I saved enough for a deposit in six months and bought my first home!"

## Portfolio Snapshot

| | |
|---|---|
| **Name** | Alice |
| **Portfolio** | 3 properties |
| **Approximate Value** | $1.25 million |
| **Total Debt** | $790,000 |
| **Net Worth (Equity)** | $460,000 |
| **Current Income** | $60,000 |

### What made you get into property investing?

Common sense. I realised that leverage and money working for me instead of me working for money was the way to go.

### What mistakes have you made?

Selling investment properties off in the past instead of holding, and striving to paying off my first property instead of leveraging to get more investment properties — I did not have the education at that time.

### What is the biggest lesson you could pass on?

Leverage! And using OPM (Other People's Money)!

### Tell us about your life before you were an investor ...

Studying at university and working part time to support myself. I started a full-time job once I graduated and was making good money working in the mines, but seemed to spend it as quickly as I made it on lifestyle, travel, car, clothes, etc. Investments were not in the picture then.

I just wanted to enjoy life and be free.

### Tell us your story of how it all started ...

It started with advice about investments from my mother when I was young. Also, my first job was working in the mines where I met a lot of older people who have worked there for years and made a lot of money but have nothing to show for it. I realised then and there that I don't want to be like them, so I saved enough for a deposit in six months and bought my first home! I kept investing, amid high and low points in my life journey.

I started investing in properties in my early twenties, and kept buying more and more, but I did listen to other people who said I was being greedy, and who asked, "How will you manage to pay them off?" I was also accused of being too materialistic and told that I should be happy with paying off my first home and that's it. Hmm ... I should have listened to myself and gotten even more properties.

## What is life like now that you are an investor?

Glorious! And my lifestyle is fantastic. I'm still accumulating properties, getting into shares investments and trying to get into an internet business while I am still employed full-time in the oil and gas industry.

I travelled to South America for a month in February 2007 and I plan to go to India in November, then off to Antarctica for Christmas.

After gaining *applied knowledge* from seminars and associating with like-minded investors, I have gotten myself back into realignment and have propelled like a torpedo!

## What is your reason for doing this? Why are you an investor?

My reason is to have financial freedom and a wealthy lifestyle through relationships, health and wellbeing.

Rather than sit and wait for the pension (yeah, right!) I am doing something about my future now and being self-sufficient and accountable for myself. I will be in the top 5% of the population, not the 95% who are not financially free.

This quote best describes my attitude: "I will do what others don't, to have a tomorrow that others won't!"

## Has anyone ever told you to "be careful" or "play it safe"? If so, how did you handle it?

I did listen to them when I was younger, but knowing what I know now, I just smile and say, "Watch me because I have applied knowledge and I am a doer, not a talker!"

## Were you or are you ever discouraged by others? If so, what happened?

When my long-term relationship broke down, I was told to sell off my joint investment properties to "get it together", so to speak. Stupidly, I did just that and to my dismay, if I would have kept them, I'd be sitting on a "gold mine". But all is not lost! Now I know what to do and am picking myself up and starting again. It is never too late to get into the property market. I don't regret the past; I just learn from the experiences so I know what to do next time.

### What words of encouragement would you give to an investor who is starting out?

Go for it and believe in yourself. Find the knowledge and education that you need. There will be others to help you in your journey.

### What do you think about the Wealth for Life strategy?

FANTASTIC! Good on you guys for making it accessible for people.

### Is there anything else you'd like to say?

Keep up the good work, and God bless.

* * *

***What did you get from reading this story?***

# Prue and Warren

"I was raised to buy a home, pay it off, pay into superannuation and really hope for the best. I never really considered my financial future."

## Portfolio Snapshot

| **Name** | Prue and Warren |
|---|---|
| **Portfolio** | 6 properties, including own home |
| **Approximate Value** | $2.1 million |
| **Total Debt** | $1.6 million |
| **Net Worth (Equity)** | $500,000 |
| **Current Income** | $115,000 |

## What made you get into property investing?

Having learned how property investing worked, it made complete sense and it is great fun!

### What mistakes have you made?

Spending a little bit of time dilly dallying and not being focused on what we wanted to achieve. We therefore lost some time by not being in the market when we could have and let opportunities go by.

### What is the biggest lesson you could pass on?

Property investing is about wealth creation. Get focused on what you want to achieve. Yes, there are expenses involved. They are business expenses and the cost of creating wealth for yourself. Keep your mind focused on wealth creation rather than fear of debt.

### Tell us about your life before you were an investor ...

**Prue:** I was raised to buy a home, pay it off, pay into superannuation and really hope for the best. I never really considered my financial future. I know now that I was leaving my financial future in other people's hands.

**Warren:** I thought the Australian dream of paying off my own home was the answer to my financial security. So I spent many years paying down the mortgage and attempting to make money by investing in the share market.

### Tell us your story of how it all started ...

Warren already had two properties when we met. We went along to one of your seminars in August 2005. It presented us with the total picture of how property investing works. Prue had a property which had considerable equity and she bought her next property by October 2005. In the next 18 months we have added two more!

### What is life like, now that you are an investor?

Life is fantastic knowing that we have taken charge of our financial future. We have a secure financial future ahead for our family and we are very close to being financially free.

### What is your reason for doing this? Why are you an investor?

We want to be financially free. We want to have a choice over what we do with our time, where and with whom we spend it.

### Has anyone ever told you to "be careful" or "play it safe"? If so, how did you handle it?

Yes, a few people. We have explained to them that for us it is safe. The history of the property market tells us that our strategy works. We have plenty of great mentors and examples that it works. All the richest people are into property and we are modelling them. Sometimes, though, you just need to end conversations.

### Were you or are you ever discouraged by others? If so, what happened?

Yes, we have been, but never in relation to property. We are very focused. We know what works and we know it is going to get us to where we want to go.

### What words of encouragement would you give to an investor who is starting out?

Keep your eye on your goal. Have faith in the future. Only listen to people who are in property investing; they will be the most helpful to you. Surround yourself with like-minded positive people. Continually educate yourself. And most of all, have a ball!

### What do you think about the Wealth for Life strategy?

Fantastic strategy. It is a fantastic feeling to know that we will be creating wealth for ourselves to use now and for generations to come.

### Is there anything else you'd like to say?

It is fantastic that you are assisting in real world education. We are most appreciative of the education we have already received from you and look forward to continuing that education and also spreading the word.

* * *

*What did you get from reading this story?*

# Thierry

"He explained to me the concept of investing using equity. I did ask him 10 million questions before being ready and since then we bought five investment properties!"

## Portfolio Snapshot

| | |
|---|---|
| **Name** | Thierry |
| **Portfolio** | 6 properties, including own home |
| **Approximate Value** | $2.2 million |
| **Total Debt** | $1.7 million |
| **Net Worth (Equity)** | $500,000 |
| **Current Income** | $135,000 |

## What made you get into property investing?

Using my equity to create wealth and because it's a long-term investment. History shows that bricks and mortar is a valuable asset.

## What mistakes have you made?

When refinancing own home and first investment property, I paid mortgage insurance on the lot instead of only on the investment property.

### What is the biggest lesson you could pass on?

Stay with this strategy. Meet the right people and get the best accountant who knows about investment property.

### Tell us about your life before you were an investor ...

I had no money left at the end of each month; I was just working to pay for food and bills.

### Tell us your story of how it all started ...

At work there was a person who was investing in property. He explained to me the concept of investing using equity. I did ask him 10 million questions before being ready and since then we've bought five investment properties!

### What is life like now that you are an investor?

I still have no money at the end of the month but have five investment properties which are working for me every day!

### What is your reason for doing this? Why are you an investor?

I am an investor to create wealth later on in my life and to become financially independent as soon as possible, with the ability to be able to pass assets to my son and daughter.

### Has anyone ever told you to "be careful" or "play it safe"? If so, how did you handle it?

Most of our friends and relatives told us this but they are old minded in that they believe you pay off your own house first and get rid of all your debts. They don't know the concept of investing using your own equity.

### Were you or are you ever discouraged by others? If so what happened?

No, I was never discouraged by other people because I was surrounded by people who wanted to create wealth. I always pursued what I wanted to do.

### What words of encouragement would you give to an investor who is starting out?

Use your equity to invest in property that will give you good long-term wealth. Compounding is the way to accelerate the process. Never, never sell property.

### What do you think about the Wealth for Life strategy?

That's what I am targeting. That's my goal and I do or try to do something to achieve it.

### Is there anything else you'd like to say?

People are excited about shares but I do not have time to look at the share market every hour or day or week. I look at my rent every month and see my property every year. That's the time I am allocating to my investments.

* * *

***What did you get from reading this story?***

## Michael and family

"I love the security that investment property brings. Knowing that property increases in value and rents go up is very reassuring! In five years' time, we won't be working more than a day a week, if that."

### Portfolio Snapshot

| **Name** | Michael |
|---|---|
| **Portfolio** | 7 properties |
| **Approximate Value** | $1.480 million |
| **Total Debt** | $832,000 million |
| **Net Worth (Equity)** | $648,000 |
| **Current Income** | $72,800 |

## What made you get into property investing?

I'm one of eight kids in my family. My mum and dad worked hard to give us life's basics. I'm the second youngest, so I saw how hard my parents worked to clothe, feed, educate and look after us. We didn't have many luxuries in life; love was the greatest thing we had. My parents struggled to keep our house in the 1980s, when interest rates were high. We lost the house. After growing up in that environment, I decided I didn't want to live that way as an adult. I purchased my first investment property when I was 21 by going half share with one of my brothers. We had no savings, I used a credit card for the minimal deposit and we were lucky enough to get vendor finance. The initial interest rate was 12.5%. The return was 11%. Rates dropped in the following years, and the property took care of itself. I've never lived in a property I owned, always rented; it was better financially. In fact, my wife owns the house we live in now!

## What mistakes have you made?

Buying my first property with absolutely no investment knowledge! The property I bought in 1994 experienced <u>no</u> capital growth in seven years! At least it was cashflow-positive, though. In the eighth and ninth year the property almost tripled in value. Glad I held onto it now. My mum rents that property from me.

The next mistake was not putting the rent up for eight years because Mum is my tenant.

I bought a well-located block of cashflow-positive flats in Toowong, Queensland, and sold them a year later for a small profit (at the time it seemed like a lot of money) before the Brisbane price boom. If we had held the property for a few more years it would have easily tripled in price and given us some great equity and income!

## What is the biggest lesson you could pass on?

Look long term, 10 years at least, and buy within 5 to 15 km of a CBD.

Buy and hold! Borrow as much as you can afford and buy as much as you can afford, as soon as you can.

### Tell us about your life before you were an investor ...

I worked two jobs and studied. Bar work at night, a couple of hours sleep in the early morning, then labouring as a tree lopper during the day. Somehow I fitted some part-time college study and university later. I was very careful with my money; I didn't spend unless it was absolutely necessary or an investment-related tax-deductible expense. I dreamed about having financial freedom, but didn't know how to get it.

### Tell us your story of how it all started ...

My brother and I both wanted to live a better life financially and not end up struggling like our parents. I was working for a boss who was an investor and who was enjoying his life. He encouraged me to buy an investment. So with those influences, no knowledge and a dream, we ventured off to buy our first investment property in 1994. Actually, we bought two the first time; we had a half share of each house. I calculated that if we could take about 11 years to pay them both off then we'd buy our next one! Later I learned about equity and leveraging.

In 1998 I bought a block of flats in Toowong, Queensland. Sold it a year later and used the cash to buy a block of cashflow-positive flats in Darwin in 2001. With the lessons from Toowong learned, I held and in 2003 used equity from my portfolio to buy a house in Darwin that saw some great growth in the following years.

### What is life like, now that you are an investor?

I love the security that investment property brings. Knowing that property increases in value and rents go up is very reassuring! In five years time we won't be working more than a day a week, if that. I'm still careful with my money, but I now spend a little on myself, my wife and our new baby. We make sure we take breaks and holidays regularly and we enjoy the things we've worked hard for.

We now have the ability to make lifestyle choices that my parents could never have dreamed of. I have travelled around the world and take an overseas trip every year (and have done so for the last nine years).

Life gets better every day!

### What is your reason for doing this? Why are you an investor?

To be able to have the lifestyle we choose and to not have to be limited by money. To be able to spend more time with my family and less time working. Investing is the easiest way to become wealthy!

### Has anyone ever told you to "be careful" or "play it safe"? If so, how did you handle it?

People who don't invest or understand investing say this. I thank them for their kind advice and make my own decisions based on research and experience.

### Were you or are you ever discouraged by others? If so what happened?

If I was, I can't remember it. I probably let it go in one ear and straight out the other.

### What words of encouragement would you give to an investor who is starting out?

If I can do it, coming from a poor background, then anyone can. Decide how you want to live your life, now, in five years, 10 years and then take action to do it, <u>now</u>! It doesn't happen overnight, but it will happen.

### What do you think about the Wealth for Life strategy?

Excellent! I have read your books over and over and watched the DVDs many times. It reinforces how easy it is to become wealthy and to live the great life you choose.

### Is there anything else you'd like to say?

I highly recommend your books and DVDs to anyone who wants to live a more financially free life. Stop worrying and start getting wealthy today!

* * *

*What did you get from reading this story?*

# Ruby

"Start young and you don't need to know everything before you start. I hadn't read an investment book or attended an investment seminar and I didn't know what LVR was until after I had six properties!"

## Portfolio Snapshot

| **Name** | Ruby |
|---|---|
| **Portfolio** | 13 properties |
| **Approximate Value** | $3 million |
| **Total Debt** | $2.3 million |
| **Net Worth (Equity)** | $700,000 |
| **Current Income** | Currently nil |

## What made you get into property investing?

I think there were a lot of reasons I went into property. I was looking for a way to make money work for me from a very young age and looking for that led me to the right people and places. My dad was a huge influence and taught me the foundations. Many of my employers also influenced me but it's not until I step back and reflect over the years that I realise how important all these people were in helping me achieve my goals.

### What mistakes have you made?

I have bought properties based on emotion rather than investment decisions. I have bought properties when I didn't have enough money to settle them. I have learned some very big lessons from these mistakes and have put systems in place to ensure they don't happen again.

### What is the biggest lesson you could pass on?

Start young and you don't need to know everything before you start — just start. I hadn't read an investment book or attended an investment seminar and I didn't know what LVR was until after I had six properties! Learn as much as you can but don't try to know it all — you *will* learn it along the way.

### Tell us about your life before you were an investor ...

I was a kid! I went through school in Bendigo in Central Victoria. I always had part-time and casual jobs from age 14. Prior to that I would babysit my cousins and wash cars at our big family functions for some pocket money. I was always a good saver and no matter how much I was earning, I always put something away each week. My parents instilled good money management in me from a young age.

### Tell us your story of how it all started ...

I was talking to my dad about building my dream home with a tennis court and pool and he told me I should buy an investment property first. I didn't know anything about buying an investment property but he told me that I could get a tenant to help me pay the mortgage and that was enough for me. It just made sense and I think it was the very next weekend that I had put in an offer for my first investment property, which I ended up buying.

I was able to negotiate with the vendor for him to throw in all of the furniture for no extra price, which allowed me to rent it out to some people from interstate who were prepared to pay more with the furniture. I had 60 days before settlement and I worked some extra shifts to help me pay for the mortgage insurance. At settlement I got a nice surprise when the bank told me they were actually capitalising the mortgage insurance so the extra money I had saved was mine to keep. Another surprise I received was that as I was earning only $5 an hour that meant I was entitled to a stamp duty refund. So within three weeks and with some extra funds in my pocket I went out and bought my second property.

Over the next couple of weekends I did some small renovations on both properties, which involved painting them and putting in new carpet, which increased the value of the properties and also allowed me to increase the rent. Using the equity I had created I bought my third property within two months. This strategy allowed me to buy two more properties over the next 12 months. By the time I had purchased my fifth property, prices were on the rise. It was the start of the boom. I headed overseas for the next 12 months while my properties were increasing in value. When I returned, four of the properties had tripled in value and one had doubled.

I had so much equity in my properties but I wasn't working at the time so found it difficult to borrow more money from the banks to purchase more property. This is when I found a mortgage broker who not only offered me a job but also helped changed my financial strategy to enable me to buy more property.

I continued to buy houses and apartments all over Australia in need of some work, organised a renovation and had them re-valued to access the equity to repeat the process. This is the strategy I still use today.

My quest for financial freedom began when I was seven years old after spending a whole day weeding my oma's garden to earn $20 (oma is Dutch for grandma). Although this was a lot of money to a seven year old, I learned a valuable lesson that day and that was: I didn't want to have to work so hard to earn money; I wanted to have money work for me.

### What is life like, now that you are an investor?

Being an investor has meant being able to do many things and have many things that I think a lot of people my age have been unable to have. I spent 12 months overseas during 2002 and 2003, mostly funded by my equity. I have taken months at a time off for trips and holidays.

I left my full-time job last year and have recently started a new business. I would never have been able to do this without having the income from my properties to support me until the business starts making money.

### What is your reason for doing this? Why are you an investor?

When I started out investing I didn't really know what I was doing. I thought initially that I could have the properties paid off by the time I was 40 and live off the rents. That strategy certainly changed along the way. I invest in property because it means I can spend my time doing what I want to do, while my properties are working for me and making me money while I sleep.

### Has anyone ever told you to "be careful" or "play it safe"? If so, how did you handle it?

When I started investing I bought three properties within five months and, as a 19-year-old, I had many people telling me I was getting in too deep and to be careful. I still get people telling me that property is risky but, like anything, there are ways to manage the risk and I look at risk management very carefully and regularly. I do listen to people as everyone is entitled to their own opinion but I make up my own mind. I'm very careful now to only take advice from those who know or who have the results I want. Often it's the people who don't really know how property works who are the ones telling you to be careful.

### Were you or are you ever discouraged by others? If so, what happened?

People used to tell me I was just lucky and it used to upset me until I heard a mentor of mine tell me what LUCK meant to him. I have adapted it slightly. L is for Location. You have to be in the right Location, like attending open-for-inspections, auctions, seminars etc. U is for Understanding. Once you are in the right location, you have to understand how the property game works, the rules of the game and your strategy.

C is for Connections. You need to have the right team around you to put the whole thing together, like real estate agents, accountants, finance brokers etc.

K is for Knowledge. Without the knowledge of what to do when the opportunity arises and the knowledge of your strategy, you will miss the opportunity.

Y is for Yield. This is where you get the returns of your hard work.

So now when people tell me I'm just lucky, I guess I am.

### What words of encouragement would you give to an investor who is starting out?

Take action and never give up. If I can do it earning $5 an hour and not knowing anything about property, anyone can do it. There is so much information available today and so many great mentors and I highly recommend people use them. But remember, you don't have to know everything! Get started as soon as you can.

### What do you think about the Wealth for Life strategy?

The Wealth for Life strategy is one of the best ways to ensure your financial future and anyone can use it.

* * *

*What did you get from reading this story?*

# David and Karen

"I have recently sold our cafe business based in Hobart, Tasmania, to pursue full-time investing ... I was diagnosed with a rare form of leukaemia and want to spend as much quality time as possible with my family while I am still able to. Having read a lot of books on investing, I knew I had no other choice."

## Portfolio Snapshot

| **Name** | David and Karen |
|---|---|
| **Portfolio** | 9 properties, including 5 joint ventures |
| **Approximate Value** | $3.447 million |
| **Total Debt** | $2.565 million |
| **Net Worth (Equity)** | $882,000 |
| **Current Income** | $200,000 |

### What made you get into property investing?

Attending a property seminar and reading books.

### What mistakes have you made?

Selling good property is one mistake. Another is not starting earlier and not acting on my better judgment to give it a go! Also, I have underestimated holding costs on off-the-plan purchases.

### What is the biggest lesson you could pass on?

Start to invest early in life and learn to minimise spending after-tax dollars. Setting up the right structures (such as a trust) prior to purchase is critically important.

### Tell us about your life before you were an investor ...

I was involved in mainly agriculture with a focus on hard work and primary production. Lots of physical work with returns very volatile depending on weather conditions and diseases, etc. The pleasure enjoyed by a rural lifestyle was certainly significant although the reward for effort and financial risk was unacceptable.

### Tell us your story of how it all started ...

I immigrated to Tasmania from Africa and soon realised I needed to have a different approach to life as all the familiar things of Africa no longer seemed to apply, or were at least not regarded as important.

I started in the mortgage industry and learned from a mentor about a line of credit and saving on interest with the use of a credit card. I borrowed and, with my own funds, bought the home we were renting. I added massive value by removing an ugly solar hot water system from the roof. This property I sold for a good tax-free profit and moved on to the next property.

Through careful buying and negotiation, I bought and sold five properties during the property wave. I simultaneously invested in several other properties, while negotiating joint venture deals with three partners. This increased my leveraging and allowed further property investing that I otherwise could not have done.

### What is life like, now that you are an investor?

I have recently sold our cafe business based in Hobart, Tasmania to pursue full-time investing. I now spend my time actively looking for properties that I can invest in, potential joint venture partners and any opportunities in the investment arena. I am also active in the stock market with strategies that supplement my income which allows me to fund the buy and hold properties until I am able to use the equity built up over time. As my local properties are all self-managed, I maintain and improve between tenants where necessary.

### What is your reason for doing this? Why are you an investor?

I was diagnosed with a rare form of leukaemia and want to spend as much quality time as possible with my family while I am still able to. Having read a lot of books on investing, I knew I had no other choice.

### Has anyone ever told you to "be careful" or "play it safe"? If so, how did you handle it?

I guess I have always told myself to "be careful, play it safe", coming from a very conservative background. Immigrating to Australia was a big risk and forced me to think outside of my square in many ways. A mentor helped me to overcome my fear of failure and to accept risk on a calculated basis.

### Were you or are you ever discouraged by others? If so, what happened?

Naysayers are plentiful. I have missed out on great opportunities because I have been unsuccessful at convincing joint ventures of a good opportunity. Such is life!

### What words of encouragement would you give to an investor who is starting out?

Moving out of your comfort zone is a scary thing to contemplate. So stop procrastinating and looking for excuses. Focus on the world of opportunity out there. Do your homework and *act*. Don't pass on, wishing you had. You don't know how much time you have left.

## What do you think about the Wealth for Life strategy?

Essential for people who want to play the game.

## Is there anything else you'd like to say?

Application of good information is the key to success. No amount of seminars or books can do it for you. You need to be able to apply good information to your unique circumstances. A mentor can be of great help in this regard.

* * *

**What did you get from reading this story?**

# Bala and Mythili

"I am feeling very confident, always open to opportunities and I've developed the ability to constantly review the situation.

The "can do" attitude has transferred to other areas of life, like my career and relationship."

## Portfolio Snapshot

| Name | Bala |
|---|---|
| **Portfolio** | 5 properties, including own home |
| **Approximate Value** | $1.8 million |
| **Total Debt** | $900,000 |
| **Net Worth (Equity)** | $900,000 |

## What made you get into property investing?

I see property as the safest way to acquire wealth through gearing.

## What mistakes have you made?

My first buy was a poor choice, the result of listening too much to the salesman.

## What is the biggest lesson you could pass on?

1. Build equity as quickly as possible in the family home.
2. Use gearing appropriately to acquire more properties but be mindful of cashflow.
3. Always stick to the low end of the scale when buying so that the effect of a downturn is minimal.

## Tell us about your life before you were an investor ...

I was very conservative and believed the saying "Never a lender nor a borrower be."

## Tell us your story of how it all started ...

I was always open to new ideas and opinions to do with investment, but it all started by attending a wealth-building seminar. The key component of that seminar was property investment and, like any other idea, you have to apply the knowledge selectively and appropriately to an individual's circumstance rather than as a whole.

## What is life like, now that you are an investor?

I am feeling very confident, always open to opportunities and I've developed the ability to constantly review the situation. The "can do" attitude has transferred to other areas of life, like my career and relationship.

## What is your reason for doing this? Why are you an investor?

1. It is a stimulating experience for the mind.
2. The urge to break out of financial dependency.

## Has anyone ever told you to "be careful" or "play it safe"? If so, how did you handle it?

Yes, people have tried to sway me into the share market due to its recent run of success. I refrained from selling out of property and instead realised the importance of a selection criteria in property investing which focuses on bridging the gap between income and expense. I am closely following the share market with a nominal capital and applying the money management principles learned through property investing.

## What words of encouragement would you give to an investor who is starting out?

Think about the bigger picture when investing in property rather than on the specific purchase. Principles of wealth building and money management should be the drivers, not the particular property being bought.

Though it is difficult initially to see sense in the following two principles of wealth, one should quickly subscribe to this gem of Eastern wisdom.

1. The purpose of wealth acquisition needs to be for benefiting the wider community rather than hoarding for personal enjoyment.

2. In setting about to create wealth, one should mimic Mother Nature which creates the things in the universe with effortless ease. What this involves is being driven by a noble purpose, doing what needs to be done with utmost discipline and accepting the result with an unquestioning attitude.

## What do you think about the Wealth for Life strategy?

It is absolutely important and a very necessary life skill. It is more important for late migrants who have to achieve wealth and independence in a shorter time. It is also vital for people transitioning into retirement, as the only thing they have at their disposal, after retirement, is the assets they've already accumulated, which they need to put to work so that they can earn a consistent income.

## Is there anything else you'd like to say?

Wealth-building training must be available at more affordable prices and as a long-term relationship concept with the investor.

* * *

***What did you get from reading this story?***

# Warren

"Property investing is for everyone BUT not everyone can invest!"

## Portfolio Snapshot

| **Name** | Warren |
|---|---|
| **Portfolio** | 6 properties |
| **Approximate Value** | $5.260 million |
| **Total Debt** | $4.046 million |
| **Net Worth (Equity)** | $1.214 million |
| **Current Income** | $183,000 |

## What made you get into property investing?

Securing financial freedom for my family. I learned early on that I need not confirm to the social norm of working for 45 years for someone else, but to learn to use what money I had.

### What mistakes have you made?

Cross collateralisation of finances and paying too much for the initial purchase price of a property, to name a few. Also, not asking the right questions from the right people.

### What is the biggest lesson you could pass on?

Learn from your mistakes and be self-guided. Everyone has an opinion on property; however, I realise now that when you want to know more, ask people that actually know more!

### Tell us about your life before you were an investor ...

Single guy with little responsibility but I knew I had to make a secure future. I started from humble beginnings, saving my pocket money weekly. I did not know why really, but liked to see the numbers increasing dollar by dollar.

### Tell us your story of how it all started ...

When I graduated, I was on about $21,000 pa — not bad for a graduate engineer. At that time I thought about how much it would take to buy a house. Basically, it did not make sense to me that as soon as you starting earning an income, you immediately go into debt for the rest of your life with no "out" in sight. I started saving hard, little by little, and then had enough to invest in something.

I decided to take control for myself and saved enough for a deposit on my first property investment in 1992 and have not looked back since.

### What is life like now that you are an investor?

I have choices now, peace of mind. I have learned to use money like a tool and treat property like a well-performing business. I have a clear strategy in place and work with expertise in the industry to continue to build a solid investment portfolio.

### What is your reason for doing this? Why are you an investor?

To secure my family's financial future. But as time goes on, I realise I can now help others avoid the same mistakes I have made and can prove that there is still some integrity in this industry.

**Has anyone ever told you to "be careful" or "play it safe"? If so, how did you handle it?**

Yes, many times. I simply say, "Yes, I am." There is no safer way to build wealth than in residential property, if you know how to structure the financing correctly and invest in reasonably good property. I am happy now that I have aligned myself with people I can rely on.

**Were you or are you ever discouraged by others? If so, what happened?**

Yes, again, many times. I would ask people why and to share their experiences to understand where they have made mistakes, so I don't do the same!

**What words of encouragement would you give to an investor who is starting out?**

It is capital that will set you financially free; use your cash to get you there. If you keep thinking you cannot afford it then you most probably never will. If you think, "How can I afford it?" your mind starts to think and you look for ways.

"Seek and you will find."

**What do you think about the Wealth for Life strategy?**

I think it works given the right guidance and applying it in the right way. But the problem is within — some people don't think about how to build wealth for life. Hence "not everyone can invest in property".

**Is there anything else you'd like to say?**

My quote: "Property investing is for everyone BUT not everyone can invest!"

* * *

*What did you get from reading this story?*

# Ernest and Susan

"When attending pre-retirement seminars, I often heard financial planners mention property investment in passing. At that time, it never occurred to me that they had a vested interest in not explaining the many forms of property investing and how they work."

### Portfolio Snapshot

| **Name** | Ernest and Susan |
|---|---|
| **Portfolio** | 6 rental properties 2 holiday letting properties 1 owner-occupied house 1 off-plan purchase pending 1 apartment contracted to purchase |
| **Approximate Value** | $4.2 million ($5 million with apartment) |
| **Total Debt** | $2.7 million |
| **Net Worth (Equity)** | $1.5 million |
| **Current Income** | $120,000 |

### What made you get into property investing?

It was chance meeting with a renowned property investor and author of several best selling property books. That was in 2000.

### What mistakes have you made?

We purchased a golf estate villa — very slow capital growth but this is about to change!

### What is the biggest lesson you could pass on?

Buy more than one property. Buy in diverse locations as close as possible to CBDs or popular centres. Use OPM as much as you can to buy as many properties as possible, in order to obtain a large portfolio, in the shortest possible time.

### Tell us about your life before you were an investor ...

I was a Commonwealth public servant who served in many parts of Australia and overseas before retiring early. I then became a taxi driver to supplement my pension.

Suzanne has been a school teacher for her entire working life.

### Tell us your story of how it all started ...

Many years ago I heard work colleagues tell their stories about rental returns and capital growth from investment property. I was always quietly curious about how they did it, but never really asked penetrating questions until I retired and had more time to pursue what had been a dormant interest. We started attending seminars which enabled us to understand what we could achieve by investing in residential property.

### What is life like, now that you are an investor?

Each year the holidays get longer and the working times become shorter! In 2006 we were able to travel the world for two months visiting Canada, Alaska, France, Switzerland, Finland, Russia, Austria and Dubai followed by a recuperative week at Margaret River, Western Australia.

## What is your reason for doing this? Why are you an investor?

So that we can enjoy life and provide a sustainable future for ourselves and our family.

## Has anyone ever told you to "be careful" or "play it safe"? If so, how did you handle it?

When we started our investment activities, our accountant warned us that we were likely to have been unwise to purchase the properties that we did. We disregarded this because (a) our purchases did not challenge our comfort levels and (b) we knew that she had a vested interest in promoting managed funds. We changed our accountant as soon as we discovered that property matters were beyond her levels of competence.

A mortgage broker once told us we were going "too fast". We pulled out of our contract on that occasion but soon found another broker who exercises his duty of care without being as prescriptive or judgmental.

## Were you or are you ever discouraged by others? If so, what happened?

When attending pre-retirement seminars, I often heard financial planners mention property investment in passing. At that time, it never occurred to me that they had a vested interest in not explaining the many forms of property investing and how they work. Property investing was simply described as something for people who like to "kick the bricks"!

I was personally advised to give priority to using my retirement benefits to repay my home mortgage and pay it off. I was therefore fortunate enough to avoid locking into a package of financial products such as allocated pensions.

## What words of encouragement would you give to an investor who is starting out?

1. In starting off, ask as many questions as needed to feel confident about the mechanics of investing.
2. Be aware of the fact that successful investing does not involve "get rich quick" answers to financial questions. Nevertheless, the

process of wealth creation works surprisingly quickly when the correct strategies are used.

3. Don't waste time dithering about whether your investments are the "best" or "optimal". Just do it safely and as soon as possible because time is your friend but procrastination is your enemy.

## What do you think about the Wealth for Life strategy?

Great, because the happiest and most productive people are likely to be those who work to live, rather than those who live to work!

## Is there anything else you'd like to say?

We're a part of a group which is highly capable of repeatedly producing a large number of successful property investors. We now buy most of our properties through this group because (1) we have tremendous gains from its properties, (2) its research is good, and (3) its ongoing support services are either free or heavily discounted.

***

***What did you get from reading this story?***

# Rob and Sharon

"Except for the first property, we have never put in any of our own money, just borrowed against the equity."

### Portfolio Snapshot

| | |
|---|---|
| **Name** | Rob and Sharon |
| **Portfolio** | 9 properties, including own home |
| **Approximate Value** | $3.7 million |
| **Total Debt** | $2 million |
| **Net Worth (Equity)** | $1.7 million |
| **Current Income** | $128,000 |

### What made you get into property investing?

We owned our house (with a mortgage) in Canberra then moved to Sydney and bought a flat to live in. After seven years in Sydney with a wife and three little kids, I had about $20k in super and two properties partly paid off. I suddenly realised at 36 years old that I had virtually nothing to fund our retirement. I knew superannuation would not be enough and surviving on a pension was out of the question. It was then that I started accumulating property to create wealth without really knowing how I was going to live off it.

### What mistakes have you made?

I've made a few! I've structured the buying of properties incorrectly buying one 95% in my name and 5% in Sharon's. Another I bought in a family trust which I now know is not the best structure from a tax perspective.

I bought a serviced apartment instead of a house in Darwin and realistically missed out on about $50–100k in extra capital gain.

I also made mistakes with finance, with all properties previously being cross collateralised. I sold our Sydney Coogee Beach unit that had fantastic views and location. And, finally, I didn't keep buying property in the late 1990s.

### What is the biggest lesson you could pass on?

Even if you don't know exactly what to buy, or how to structure it, just buy what you think is best at the time. By the time you work out the best way to buy property that suits your knowledge, skills and comfort factor, you would have missed out on probably your first million in capital gain.

### Tell us about your life before you were an investor ...

My second career was running a very busy family motel in Glebe, Sydney. During that time our three kids were born and Sharon was also working at the motel. We were just running out of hours in the day, and not spending enough family time, so we packed up and moved back to Canberra. In Canberra we gave our tenant notice, moved in, got regular jobs, and then after a while started thinking about the future again.

### Tell us your story of how it all started ...

We had an ex-government three-bedroom home in Canberra and a two-bedroom apartment in Coogee. Our family of five needed a bigger house so we sold both and bought our current home mortgage free in 1996. Later in 1999 we had enough for a deposit for one three-bed apartment in Canberra. I tried online share trading for a while, but there was a lot of effort for little overall gain (probably because I wasn't very good at it).

Then I realised the apartment was going well, so I started buying more apartments in Canberra in 2001. We bought about one every six months until we had five and the bank said we couldn't borrow any more. These were easy to buy as the yields were good. We started buying again in 2004 after learning more about finance strategies and we also changed brokers. Except for the first property, we have never put in any of our own money, just borrowed against the equity.

## What is life like, now that you are an investor?

Sharon and I are still working. We now have additional money from investments that have enabled us to spend $30k on renovating the kitchen, $8k on a family trip to Fiji, $30k on a new car, $80k on the backyard including a lovely in-ground pool, $10k last school holidays on a family holiday sailing a boat around the Whitsundays. All of this in the last five years!

In the last 10 years we have pretty much just lived fairly comfortably on our salaries and don't save any money. It's our investments that have enabled us to have a lifestyle that would probably need much more stressful jobs with nearly double the salary to live like this.

## What is your reason for doing this? Why are you an investor?

It's all about leverage. There's no way that superannuation would fund the lifestyle we want in retirement unless we both worked full time until age 65. Taking second jobs was out of the question, so we had to work smarter and use the leverage of the equity we had to build more income-producing assets.

The extra bonus now is that we are partly living off our equity to give us a better lifestyle now, instead of waiting until we give up our day jobs. My main goal now is to get to $5m in assets and $2m in equity, which I believe will be the decision point to give up our current jobs and maybe move to part-time, less stressful jobs, while the youngest boy is still at school.

## Has anyone ever told you to "be careful" or "play it safe"? If so, how did you handle it?

I usually don't talk about investing unless someone else brings it up or I already know they invest or run a business. When people tell me to "play it safe" or say that "they could never do that", I just briefly tell them my story —

how I started with not knowing much, built up my portfolio and plan to use my investments instead of waiting for superannuation or the pension.

### Were you or are you ever discouraged by others? If so, what happened?

In early days it was more often people trying to encourage me in different directions, for example, to buy serviced apartments. It's only in the last year or two that I became comfortable in knowing exactly what property I want to buy next and what I wanted to do with shares.

### What words of encouragement would you give to an investor who is starting out?

1. Educate yourself. Go to all the free seminars and the ones that charge a nominal $60 or so. Subscribe to property magazines and surf the internet for property education websites.
2. Work towards buying your first property as soon as possible.
3. Just buy the best property you think is right for you at the time. This is the quickest way to learn.

### What do you think about the Wealth for Life strategy?

This should be taught in every secondary school. I think a national youth group movement (like Scouts, YMCA, etc) should be started that teaches this information.

### Is there anything else you'd like to say?

Please keep educating everyone!

* * *

*What did you get from reading this story?*

# Rob and Moya

"At the ripe age of 41, we went bankrupt ... We had our cars towed away, had to hand in the keys to our home, the bailiff was even trying to take my wedding ring ... With three children, it wasn't easy."

## Portfolio Snapshot

| **Name** | Moya and Rob |
|---|---|
| **Portfolio** | 14 properties |
| **Approximate Value** | $7 million |
| **Total Debt** | $5 million |
| **Net Worth (Equity)** | $2 million |
| **Current Income** | $260,000 including hubby and son |

## What made you get into property investing?

I read many books and realised that to become wealthy we had to get into property. I went one step forward and became a real estate representative so that I could gain the knowledge needed when buying.

## What mistakes have you made?

Selling some of our properties when we really didn't need to.

Working too hard in my day-to-day job and losing sight of where we have made our money, which is property investing. Now knowing what is important, I have semi-retired.

## What is the biggest lesson you could pass on?

Don't listen to people who haven't done it; instead, listen to the people who have!

## Tell us about your life before you were an investor ...

At the ripe age of 41, we went bankrupt. (It was through a family business. My husband had nothing to do with it, but because he was married to me, everything we had built together, he lost as well.) We had our cars towed away, had to hand in the keys to our home; the bailiff was even trying to take my wedding ring! Knowing the bailiff was coming, we had a removalist truck come and pick up our furniture and park down the street until they left. With three children, it wasn't easy.

I started Nutri-Metics, where I learned what goals were, and because I didn't have a car (I bought my sister-in-law's old bomb to get around). I knew I could achieve one through Nutri-Metics, which I did! All the time my husband was working hard as a bricklayer.

This is when I read the books and decided to become a real estate agent to understand more about property. I failed the course, sat for it again and passed. The following year I received rookie of the year for the whole of Western Australia (WA) and the following year I was number 2 in sales for the whole of WA!

Let me tell you, there's a lot more to this story!

## Tell us your story of how it all started ...

I had been in real estate for two years when I suggested to our son that he needed to get into property (as he works in the mines) and not waste his money. So our first property was with him.

Being in the "game", I saw a lot of bargains and gained a huge amount of knowledge and this knowledge was what we needed to keep going. The big picture became very clear.

My husband went to Ireland to work for three months and I bought two canal blocks; I sold one before settlement as we couldn't afford it, and built on the other. This gave us a good start.

The way we think now really started a year ago, when we attended some seminars and read books on property, and your books and DVDs too.

It changed my mindset; so really this is when I started to do things differently, and it is working.

### What is life like now that you are an investor?

I have a balance in my life which I never had before and I don't worry about the next dollar. Also, meeting like-minded people is fantastic and I'm gaining knowledge every day. And being able to share this knowledge is wonderful as it is also helping other people achieve too.

Life is fantastic!

### What is your reason for doing this? Why are you an investor?

I love what I do. I love to show people what we do and show that it can be done. If we can do it, anyone can. People need to realise that you are never too old or that you don't have enough to start with. You just have to start!

I love to share my knowledge and show people "how" you can become wealthy just by changing your mindset.

My other reason is to educate my children and have them set up for life.

### Has anyone ever told you to "be careful" or "play it safe"? If so, how did you handle it?

Nearly everyone and I don't listen to them as I know better.

### Were you or are you ever discouraged by others? If so, what happened?

An example was when I was going to attend a seminar last year and people at work were trying to talk me out of it because of the price, but this seminar changed our life.

When I came back, I held a mini seminar with friends, showing your DVDs. I now encourage many people to just try, and some of them are now on their way to becoming wealthy too!

### What words of encouragement would you give to an investor who is starting out?

Listen to people who have done it. Read, educate your mind. Knowledge is power! Don't procrastinate, just start. You are not alone and if you feel you are, find a mentor.

Never give up, learn by your mistakes. Remember, it's a test as it will make you grow; things happen for a reason.

### What do you think about the Wealth for Life strategy?

I love it! It has given us a life, freedom and the enjoyment of helping others. I am truly passionate about what I do.

### Is there anything else you'd like to say?

It's all about your mindset. And remember: You are never too old and you don't need a lot of money to start!

***

***What did you get from reading this story?***

# Greg

"I had the best education you can get (PhD) and a top government job with great potential, but no prospects of generating wealth by just working."

## Portfolio Snapshot

| **Name** | Greg |
|---|---|
| **Portfolio** | 1 property |
| **Approximate Value** | $2.5 million |
| **Total Debt** | $400,000 |
| **Net Worth (Equity)** | $2.1 million |
| **Current Income** | $50,000 |

## What made you get into property investing?

Mum always said, "Buy a house and let the tenants pay it off. All you need is the deposit and the house will be yours."

### What mistakes have you made?

I sold properties to reduce debt. I tried to find out about where I could borrow to service debt in the short term, but couldn't get the information I needed.

What I had was a loan for just on $500,000 and four properties, three of which were mortgaged. I was paying around $30,000 per year in interest on the loan. There was a problem renting out my houses at this time (around 1992) and my cashflow was reduced because I couldn't get tenants and my wife had stopped working to have our first child. I thought, "If I sold the unmortgaged property (which was worth about $120,000) and put the money in a bank account I could draw on this for about four years to pay the interest on the remaining three properties."

I was hoping to "buy time" with the sale proceeds of one of my properties so that I could hold on to the remaining three properties. I felt sure that within the four years the $120,000 sales proceeds would last, renters would return to the market and my cashflow would be re-established.

Obviously, this buying time concept, which you teach in your seminars, really works, but back in 1992 when I first hit on the idea, I had never had it explained to me by someone who had employed it. In the end, I didn't have the nerve to do it. I sold three of my four properties and got out of debt. This was my biggest mistake.

### What is the biggest lesson you could pass on?

Never sell property. Be persistent in getting the best advice on how to achieve your goals.

### Tell us about your life before you were an investor ...

I had the best education you can get (PhD) and a top government job with great potential, but no prospects of generating wealth by just working. Mum told me when I was a boy that you can never get rich just working for someone else. I saved all I could, which was a lot, but inflation always seemed to beat me. For many years I tried unsuccessfully to bridge the deposit gap to get my first house.

### Tell us your story of how it all started ...

My break came when Mum and Dad gave me a few thousand dollars to bridge the deposit gap so I could buy my first home; I was 30. I bought my first home in Ermington, NSW. It cost $70,000, and I had a deposit of $15,000. At this time I ended up (after outgoings on my loan) with $20 per week. This was hardly enough to buy petrol and food. About eight months after I bought my first home, my mother died, so I moved back with my father to look after him; he was 76 and not in good health.

At this point I was now an investor because I rented out my home and, with the tax benefits, I found my cash surplus was now in excess of $200 per week. I saved around $12,000 in the 18 months that I was back with Dad and had a loan offer that I had applied for two years earlier suddenly presented to me. The catch was that I had only three months to take it up, and if I didn't, I would revert back to the end of the waiting list, which by this time was five years long. When I first applied for this loan, the waiting time was one to two years. I took the loan and bought a house in Merrylands, NSW, which cost $60,000. My cashflow position was the same, if not better, with the tax advantages of having two investment properties.

### What is life like now that you are an investor?

My lifestyle improved greatly as an investor. My income went up and my taxes went down. I had peace of mind and was actually saving lots of cash in the bank. The increase in equity from the growth of my properties gave me such peace of mind that I started spending and enjoying my money, with the knowledge that my spending was not reducing my assets. I travelled overseas and had a go at some other business ventures.

### What is your reason for doing this? Why are you an investor?

My initial reason was the fact that I witnessed property prices constantly increasing and that individuals who owned property were generating wealth for themselves while those who rented didn't. I could see that what my mother had told me as a child was correct: "Put a deposit on a house and the tenants pay it off for you." By the time I was 30, I had lived to see my parents' house increase in value from $4000 to $80,000.

I also wanted to generate wealth to pass on to my children (assuming I was going to get married and have some) as I didn't want them to have to go through the deposit gap worries that I had experienced. Most importantly, I wanted something better for my children — financial freedom which would release them from the slavery imposed by having to work for a boss who might be unbearable, as I eventually experienced.

### Has anyone ever told you to "be careful" or "play it safe"? If so, how did you handle it?

Yes, and I didn't take much notice of it after seeing what that approach had done to my father and our family. My dad was given all the authoritative advice from his old-maid sisters and friends; you know the type — people who have never done anything or owned anything. Dad paid dearly for taking that advice; he ended up with a fraction of what he should have had if he only ignored such advice.

### Were you or are you ever discouraged by others? If so, what happened?

Yes, I have been, but I doubt if I ever will be again. There were times when I had the knowledge to act but wanted reassurance from those around me and so I didn't act. Examples include not borrowing $100,000 to put into some shares when they went down to $7 per share. I knew they would bounce back, but my wife said she wouldn't be able to sleep at night. Six months later the shares went up to $14. I was keen on buying 20,000 shares in another company at $2 per share after they had dropped from around $30 per share; I asked my brother for his opinion as he had some knowledge on stock and he said he wouldn't touch them with a barge pole. This put me off what I knew was a sure winner; 12 months later the shares were around $15 each. I have learned the hard way and the expensive way: when you know something is right, don't seek advice from people who know nothing on the subject. Act on your own expertise.

### What words of encouragement would you give to an investor who is starting out?

Take responsibility for your own actions. Always try and learn more; never stop learning. Seek knowledge or good advice from experts who have a proven track record. In real estate, a person's expertise or qualifications should be gauged by how much real estate that person owns, not by their university degrees, diplomas or technical certificates. Never sell real estate, buy and hold. I've learned that expensive lesson the hard way!

You're never too old to be an investor. Don't fall into the trap of being a miser; spend some of your wealth to have a good lifestyle while still investing. Don't expect wealth to come instantly; it takes time but once you start generating it, then the rate at which it comes will increase. Start building wealth as soon as you can or as young as you can but don't let your age hinder you; you're never too old to start. Wealth creation is a lifelong process as should be the acquisition of knowledge. It can be fun and gives your life purpose. With wealth and knowledge you can help others rather than being dependent upon others; this can add to your quality of life.

Don't allow caution to develop into procrastination. If you really want to be an investor, then you need to write down your goals and prepare a to-do list to achieve those goals. Start doing each task methodically; having a go and persistence is the key to success.

### What do you think about the Wealth for Life strategy?

I am encouraged by it and I am actively (but slowly) working on implementing this strategy and trying to teach it to my children.

### Is there anything else you'd like to say?

If you want people to do things and to succeed at what they do you must motivate them and keep them motivated during the entire course of whatever it is that they are doing. Motivation can be achieved by many things, including developing a passion for something, giving rewards along the way, providing a sense of worth and achievement. There have been hundreds of books written by dozens of people on how to become wealthy; why then do we still have poor people? Like the old saying: "You can lead a horse to water, but you can't make it drink."

Many people are very well-off or wealthy and don't know it. I know a local man who is retired and catches the train every day at 8.30 a.m. He sits around in the main street and occasionally asks people for money, which he spends on alcohol at the pub. I first met him when I used to catch the train into the city where I worked. He was always there catching the train at 8.30 a.m. He catches the 4.30 p.m. train back to our station and occasionally if I was on my way home at this time I would see him.

One day when I was walking with my wife and children, I saw this gentleman. I took the opportunity to talk with him and I learned a bit about him. Although he dressed in a suit, it was not well kept. It turned out that he owned and lived in a house near our station. His house would be worth well in excess of $700,000 but he had no idea of its worth or how he could tap into his wealth. If he knew how and was willing, he could tap into his $700,000 wealth to give himself a very nice lifestyle in his declining years.

When this chap dies, the government will end up with his wealth. I know several people in this position of being asset rich and cash poor. It seems a shame that the government doesn't have the facilities to help these people to have a good lifestyle in their last few years by helping them benefit from their assets rather than just taking those assets when they die. People who are asset rich and cash poor are that way largely because they were indoctrinated by their parents to save and be frugal, with the result that their wealth creation has been successful, but without any useful purpose or meaning. Why create wealth if you don't intend to use it? If you keep putting off when you will use your wealth then you may find that you die and end up as the richest person in the cemetery. If you do not have a reason for generating wealth then why bother to generate it? You should keep in mind your reason for generating wealth and exactly how you need to achieve what you set out to do. For me, an important question to ask yourself every day is, "Am I happy?" If not, do something about it.

* * *

***What did you get from reading this story?***

# Bob and Pat

"We walk to work, have breakfast at a beach suburb on weekends and look at the Sydney Opera House from our lounge room ...We enjoy travelling and like to have the freedom to do so. Also, we'd like to have the ability to help the community."

## Portfolio Snapshot

| | |
|---|---|
| **Name** | Bob and Pat |
| **Portfolio** | Property \$3.8 million Shares \$1.2 million Superannuation \$600,000 |
| **Approximate Value** | \$5.6 million |
| **Total Debt** | \$2.2 million |
| **Net Worth (Equity)** | \$3.6 million |
| **Current Income** | We salary-sacrifice all our salaries |

## What made you get into property investing?

I first read a book in the late '80s which explained property cycles; this made sense to me so I started investing.

## What mistakes have you made?

Instead of buying property directly, I purchased income streams via lease options in Brisbane. Although they were positively geared investments, I also factored in capital growth of 5% compounded annually. I did this to entice future purchasers; this was 3% lower than the historical capital growth of the area if I'd purchased directly. By selling, I lost the ability to tap into future equity. I also purchased rural positively geared property. I don't like rural property as I have found there is very little equity growth.

## What is the biggest lesson you could pass on?

Buy blue chip property and shares. Someone told me that property is for growth and shares are for income. It is so true. I have always abided by the philosophy of pay now play later. Also, you will find that people get jealous. There is no need to be jealous; find out how they structured things and do it yourself. It is not how much you earn but what you do with it.

## Tell us about your life before you were an investor ...

I spent 20 years in the navy and put our daughters through private Catholic schools. I started when I was 40 years of age (now 56) and have been with the Department of Defence for 39 years. One of our daughters is now a National Institute of Dramatic Arts graduate and the other works for an advertising firm in Sydney.

## Tell us your story of how it all started ...

I purchased a property in Woden, ACT, in 1991 just before the Liberal government downsized the public service. I still have it.

After the downsize in Canberra, the rental market was reassessed and hence rents dropped; tenants were hard to get as people shifted interstate. I then started looking at lease options that provided positive income to offset the loss of income in Canberra. I purchased a number of lease options in Brisbane. They were structured for a three-year interest-only loan, giving the future purchaser the option to purchase at the end of the three-year mark. I factored in 2% over the current annual interest rate and paid interest in advance each June. All the purchases settled or settled early. As I explained earlier, in hindsight, that was a mistake due to lost future equity. I would like that equity now as I am in the process of refinancing and that will take our share portfolio to $2 million. I also missed a number of buying opportunities in Canberra, but early in your investing career it takes guts to purchase in a down market. I guess the bottom line is that blue chip property and blue chip shares are the safest bet in town. Anyway I battled on — here I am; please pass the beer nuts.

### What is life like now that you are an investor?

My wife and I live in the Sydney CBD in rental accommodation; it's a high-rise apartment in the middle of Sydney with heated pool, sauna etc. We walk to work, have breakfast at a beach suburb on weekends and gaze at the Sydney Opera House from our lounge room. We pay the rent (some of which is tax-deductible due to one of the bedrooms being an office) from the share dividends received. Our salaries are 95% salary-sacrificed to a non-government superannuation fund, and 5% goes into a government superannuation fund.

### What is your reason for doing this? Why are you an investor?

The reason is we're planning for our retirement. We enjoy travelling and like to have the freedom to do so. We do one international trip per year. It is nice sitting around the pool in Bangkok knowing the little bees (property) are making honey. Also, we like the choice to have the ability to help our daughters and the community.

### Has anyone ever told you to "be careful" or "play it safe"? If so, how did you handle it?

I don't think anyone really listens to us; you just have to learn those lessons yourself and play the cards you are dealt. I think it is more important to not give up because everyone loses money or could have done better at some point. Property is, however, very forgiving if you give it time. I always have believed that if you are into shares or property then you will have a comfortable retirement. Do anything, just do something.

### Were you or are you ever discouraged by others? If so, what happened?

People have tried to discourage me all my life. They have said, "Don't worry about promotional courses, there are not enough vacancies" or "Don't invest in property, it can't get any more expensive" and the best: "Why don't you relax and enjoy life?" ... Well, my wife and I certainly are now!

### What words of encouragement would you give to an investor who is starting out?

Never, never, never give up. Did I say never? As I said earlier, just do *something.*

### What do you think about the Wealth for Life strategy?

What can I say — it works.

* * *

***What did you get from reading this story?***

# 12

# Getting Help with Your Next Step ...

Successful application of the Wealth for Life strategy requires the following:

## 1. THE RIGHT MINDSET

When we mention mindset we're talking about how you think with regards to finances, debt, the property market and money in general. Having the right mindset is the first and most important requirement of this strategy.

## 2. APPROPRIATE ASSET CLASS

Of course, we believe property to be the most appropriate asset class, but that's not because we like property. Rather, it's because:

1. It has a proven track record.
2. It can be used to borrow money.

If there was another asset that provided a better track record and the same borrowing capacity then that would be a better asset class in our opinion.

## 3. SAFETY

A safety factor should be built into any investment strategy. The W4L safety factor is ensuring that there is enough of a time buffer to last until the next property cycle.

Also, insurances such as life insurance, income protection and property insurance need to be considered to provide further safety nets. To arrange this, you need to speak with a qualified financial advisor.

## 4. STRUCTURE

Using the right structure, such as a trust, provides further safety in the form of asset protection and certain tax benefits. For more information on this topic, we recommend you read *How to Legally Reduce Your Tax ... without losing any money!*

## 5. PROFESSIONAL TEAM

A professional team is vital to successfully implementing this strategy. Just like any professional athlete needs a coach, so too do Players. Having professionals in the areas of accounting, finance and the different property markets greatly improves your results and speed of progress. If you don't have a team of professionals or you feel that your current team of advisors is holding you back, then you may want to visit Chan & Naylor. Full details on the different consultations available are on the last page of this book or on our website.

## FEEDBACK: WE'RE HAPPY TO HEAR FROM OUR READERS

For us to provide education that is applicable to you and your future needs, we ask that you take the time to give us some feedback.

In a constantly changing world, it's important that we fully understand your different individual situations and the issues that may be preventing or slowing your progress on your way to wealth. Knowledge of topics such as tax, finance, money management and business, to name a few, are all vital to ensuring and speeding your progress towards financial independence.

## SUCCESS

Also, let us know what you've learned from reading this book and applying its methods and tools; tell us about your successes by sending an email via the **Ask Us** section of the website. We are very passionate about people applying this material and would love to hear about any successes you have, big or small.

**FINAL WORD**

At **Chan & Naylor**, we realise that becoming financially independent requires knowledge, experience and, every now and then, some guidance. Therefore, our purpose is:

To teach every Australian how to become a real Player by providing applicable education, ethical advice and resources that increase investment returns and fast track their Road to Wealth.

Although we use the term "fast track", it is not a matter of getting rich quick; speed has more to do with sensible planning and the application of known principles and techniques. Our experience has shown that most overnight successes are not an overnight success at all; they're preceded by years of learning.

And that is our final message. Keep on learning, as knowledge is, in the end, your greatest asset. And no matter what happens, treat investing, money and life as a game and that way, despite any ups and downs, you will have fun. And isn't that what we are here for after all ...?

# 13

# The Wealth for Life Factors

1. Wealth accumulation is a game.
2. A trader is one who buys and sells; an investor is one who accumulates.
3. *Wealth for Life* is a game for investors.
4. Always check people's opinions against actual facts and make your own judgment.
5. Take note of vested interests — does an individual personally gain from the advice they give?
6. An independent lender's willingness to lend is an indicator of their confidence in the asset.
7. Median property prices in Australia have, on average, doubled every 10 years since 1901.
8. "Time in the market" is more important than "timing the market".
9. Supply and demand drives property prices.

10. Supply and demand are driven by the following:

    1. The amount of land available in places where people want to live.

    2. The number of properties being built in those areas.

    3. The number of people needing a place to live.

    4. The ability to get finance.

    5. Affordability.

11. Selling costs you money.

12. You don't have to sell to access your profits.

13. As a rule of thumb, selling and reinvesting can cost about 20% of the asset value.

14. Growth and yield is only half the picture.

15. The size of your assets matters.

16. ROI is improved with *more* debt.

17. An investor should use other people's money before their own.

18. Debt is only risky if you can't get more debt.

19. The Player focuses on increasing their asset base, not on reducing their debt.

20. Keep it safe.

21. The Player ensures they can weather the storm.

22. The Wealth for Life strategy works in areas where property prices increase over time.

23. Property prices will continue to rise in areas of demand.

24. The areas where people *need* and *want* to live will be in demand.

25. Finance needs to be in place and constantly reviewed.

26. Wealth for Life is not about buying real estate, it's about *buying time.*

## Endnotes

1 CGT 50% Discount Assumed

2 Deduct $30,000 University fee from Net Proceed from Sale of Property.

3 equity: difference between the value of an asset and the amount owed on that asset; asset value less the debt.

4 loan to lalue ratio (LVR): the loan amount compared to the asset value represented as a percentage. The formula is (loan/asset value) × 100 = LVR%.

# Appendix

## Sydney Median Property Prices from 1901 to 2006

| Period Ending | Median Value | Period Ending | Median Value | Period Ending | Median Value | Period Ending | Median Value | Period Ending | Median Value |
|---|---|---|---|---|---|---|---|---|---|
| 30/06/01 | 1,071 | 30/06/42 | 1,665 | 30/06/80 | 62,207 | 30/09/90 | 173,959 | 31/12/00 | 337,598 |
| 30/06/02 | 1,020 | 30/06/43 | 1,762 | 30/09/80 | 65,823 | 31/12/90 | 178,288 | 31/03/01 | 346,065 |
| 30/06/03 | 928 | 30/06/44 | 1,600 | 31/12/80 | 68,784 | 31/03/91 | 177,165 | 30/06/01 | 357,242 |
| 30/06/04 | 881 | 30/06/45 | 1,623 | 31/03/81 | 71,354 | 30/06/91 | 179,677 | 30/09/01 | 379,096 |
| 30/06/05 | 1,113 | 30/06/46 | 2,041 | 30/06/81 | 71,724 | 30/09/91 | 184,446 | 31/12/01 | 400,753 |
| 30/06/06 | 928 | 30/06/47 | 2,783 | 30/09/81 | 73,394 | 31/12/91 | 181,525 | 31/03/02 | 414,593 |
| 30/06/07 | 1,173 | 30/06/48 | 4,257 | 31/12/81 | 73,859 | 31/03/92 | 183,096 | 30/06/02 | 447,830 |
| 30/06/08 | 1,159 | 30/06/49 | 5,287 | 31/03/82 | 74,379 | 30/06/92 | 183,215 | 30/09/02 | 469,053 |
| 30/06/09 | 1,020 | 30/06/50 | 5,101 | 30/06/82 | 72,361 | 30/09/92 | 189,849 | 31/12/02 | 488,818 |
| 30/06/10 | 1,285 | 30/06/51 | 6,307 | 30/09/82 | 71,165 | 31/12/92 | 186,857 | 31/03/03 | 496,061 |
| 30/06/11 | 1,067 | 30/06/52 | 5,982 | 31/12/82 | 69,968 | 31/03/93 | 187,809 | 30/06/03 | 513,726 |
| 30/06/12 | 1,368 | 30/06/53 | 5,324 | 31/03/83 | 71,446 | 30/06/93 | 188,361 | 30/09/03 | 551,077 |
| 30/06/13 | 1,577 | 30/06/54 | 6,446 | 30/06/83 | 71,648 | 30/09/93 | 194,809 | 31/12/03 | 565,141 |
| 30/06/14 | 1,252 | 30/06/55 | 7,095 | 30/09/83 | 72,072 | 31/12/93 | 194,167 | 31/03/04 | 563,205 |
| 30/06/15 | 1,206 | 30/06/56 | 7,049 | 31/12/83 | 73,862 | 31/03/94 | 201,910 | 30/06/04 | 555,249 |
| 30/06/16 | 1,350 | 30/06/57 | 7,165 | 31/03/84 | 76,605 | 30/06/94 | 207,558 | 30/09/04 | 546,359 |
| 30/06/17 | 1,507 | 30/06/58 | 8,023 | 30/06/84 | 77,537 | 30/09/94 | 212,444 | 31/12/04 | 545,110 |
| 30/06/18 | 1,855 | 30/06/59 | 7,791 | 30/09/84 | 78,799 | 31/12/94 | 212,296 | 31/03/05 | 545,434 |
| 30/06/19 | 1,530 | 30/06/60 | 8,709 | 31/12/84 | 81,454 | 31/03/95 | 210,194 | 30/06/05 | 533,144 |
| 30/06/20 | 1,948 | 30/06/61 | 8,765 | 31/03/85 | 81,324 | 30/06/95 | 209,790 | 30/09/05 | 533,145 |
| 30/06/21 | 2,017 | 30/06/62 | 8,348 | 30/06/85 | 83,080 | 30/09/95 | 210,450 | 31/12/05 | 532,000 |
| 30/06/22 | 2,087 | 30/06/63 | 8,997 | 30/09/85 | 84,339 | 31/12/95 | 211,898 | 31/03/06 | 524,300 |
| 30/06/23 | 1,948 | 30/06/64 | 8,811 | 31/12/85 | 85,566 | 31/03/96 | 212,359 | 30/06/06 | 520,300 |
| 30/06/24 | 2,180 | 30/06/65 | 9,646 | 31/03/86 | 86,752 | 30/06/96 | 217,103 | 30/03/07 | 549,000 |
| 30/06/25 | 1,948 | 30/06/66 | 9,925 | 30/06/86 | 87,292 | 30/09/96 | 221,029 | 30/06/07 | 569,000 |
| 30/06/26 | 1,948 | 30/06/67 | 10,667 | 30/09/86 | 89,967 | 31/12/96 | 225,501 | 30/03/08 | 584,000 |
| 30/06/27 | 1,716 | 30/06/68 | 11,594 | 31/12/86 | 91,384 | 31/03/97 | 227,913 | 30/06/08 | 573,000 |
| 30/06/28 | 1,716 | 30/06/69 | 12,985 | 31/03/87 | 96,638 | 30/06/97 | 240,449 | 30/03/09 | 565,000 |
| 30/06/29 | 1,948 | 30/06/70 | 14,006 | 30/06/87 | 99,296 | 30/09/97 | 248,161 | 30/05/09 | 574,000 |
| 30/06/30 | 1,665 | 30/06/71 | 17,498 | 30/09/87 | 106,062 | 31/12/97 | 256,405 | 30/03/10 | 641,000 |
| 30/06/31 | 1,484 | 30/06/72 | 18,528 | 31/12/87 | 117,711 | 31/03/98 | 260,176 | 30/05/10 | 657,500 |
| 30/06/32 | 1,594 | 30/06/73 | 24,580 | 31/03/88 | 127,369 | 30/06/98 | 271,068 | 30/03/11 | 670,000 |
| 30/06/33 | 1,665 | 30/06/74 | 27,687 | 30/06/88 | 149,508 | 30/09/98 | 269,231 | 30/05/11 | 667,500 |
| 30/06/34 | 1,836 | 30/06/75 | 29,542 | 30/09/88 | 163,232 | 31/12/98 | 280,041 | 30/03/12 | 668,000 |
| 30/06/35 | 1,660 | 30/06/76 | 29,960 | 31/12/88 | 175,052 | 31/03/99 | 281,236 | 30/05/12 | 675,500 |
| 30/06/36 | 1,623 | 30/06/77 | 34,064 | 31/03/89 | 183,745 | 30/06/99 | 295,568 | 30/03/13 | 694,000 |
| 30/06/37 | 1,475 | 30/06/78 | 36,615 | 30/06/89 | 180,561 | 30/09/99 | 303,330 | 30/05/13 | 701,500 |
| 30/06/38 | 1,577 | 30/06/79 | 45,102 | 30/09/89 | 175,144 | 31/12/99 | 318,012 | 30/03/14 | 795,500 |
| 30/06/39 | 1,623 | 30/09/79 | 51,037 | 31/12/89 | 177,176 | 31/03/00 | 325,471 | 30/05/14 | 824,000 |
| 30/06/40 | 1,623 | 31/12/79 | 53,668 | 31/03/90 | 179,767 | 30/06/00 | 335,478 | 30/03/15 | 929,000 |
| 30/06/41 | 1,855 | 31/03/80 | 59,358 | 30/06/90 | 175,005 | 30/09/00 | 329,932 | 30/05/15 | 961,500 |
| 30/03/16 | $1,043,000 | 30/03/17 | $1,129,500 | 30/03/18 | $1,144,000 | | | | |
| 30/05/16 | $1,050,000 | 30/05/17 | $1,136,000 | 30/05/18 | $1,136,000 | | | | |

Source: Residex/DPN

# Glossary

| | |
|---|---|
| **ABN** | Australian Business Number. All businesses need this to be able to claim their GST expenses. |
| **Aggressive** | In the finance sense, characterised by a willingness to accept above-average risk in pursuit of above-average returns. |
| **All Ordinaries** | The index is made up of the share prices of about 500 of the largest Australian companies. Established by the Australian Stock Exchange at 500 points in January 1980, it is the predominant measure of the overall performance of the Australian share market. The companies are adjusted in value according to the total market value of their shares. Often abbreviated to All Ords. |
| **Appreciation** | An increase in price or value. |
| **Asset** | A standard dictionary describes an asset as a possession, a thing of value. In the investing world an asset is something that increases your wealth, either by cashflow or capital gain. |
| **ATO** | Australian Taxation Office is the main revenue collection agency, and is part of the Treasurer's portfolio. Its role is to design and manage systems that fund services for Australians. |
| **Baby Boomers** | Those born after the Second World War between the late 1940s and 1960s. This group makes up a large percentage of the population. |

| | |
|---|---|
| **Balance Sheet** | The list of your assets and liabilities. Used to calculate the net worth of a person or organisation (net worth = total assets – total liabilities). See net worth in this glossary. |
| **Beneficial Ownership** | Allowing a person to enjoy the benefits of ownership (including usage, income, profits, etc) even though legal title is in another name. |
| **Beneficiary** | The person who is entitled to the assets and income of a trust. |
| **Brokerage** | The fee paid for the buying or selling of something. Normally associated with the buying and selling of shares. |
| **Bubble** | A risky or unreliable business or speculative plan, especially one proving to be fraudulent or unsuccessful. |
| **Capital** | Wealth in the form of money or property owned by a person or business. |
| **Capital Gain** | The value an asset increases by. If a house is purchased for $100,000 and is re-valued at $140,000, it has a capital gain of $40,000. |
| **Capital Gains Tax** | Capital gains tax is the tax imposed on an asset that has increased in value and is sold. |
| **Cashflow** | The movement of money received and spent; the pattern of income and expenses. |
| **Commissioner** | A government administrator. In this book it refers specifically to the Commissioner of Taxation of the ATO. |
| **Company** | A legal entity that is recognised by the ATO and therefore has its own tax and legal laws, which differ from those laws imposed on individuals. |
| **Compliance** | The work performed by an accountant to ensure you have followed the laws in regards to taxation. Literally means to submit. |
| **Compounding** | Adding to the original amount, making it larger. |
| **Conveyancing** | Transferring of the legal title of the property. |

| | |
|---|---|
| **Corporation** | Another name for a company. |
| **Cross Collateralisation** | Where the collateral (security) of a single loan is guaranteed by more than one asset (usually property). |
| **Deed** | A signed document that outlines the terms of an agreement. |
| **Depreciation** | A decrease in price or value. |
| **Director** | The role in a company where the person is responsible for the direction and performance of the company.<br>A company can have many directors. |
| **Dividends** | Profits of a company that are distributed to its shareholders; usually paid quarterly. |
| **Due Diligence** | The process of checking and double-checking that an investment or a company is worth what the owner or seller says it is. It involves analysis of the Profit and Loss, balance sheet, and cashflow statements. Often conducted by qualified accountants, although every investor needs to understand this process and realise all investing requires due diligence. |
| **Entity** | A separate structure such as a trust or company. |
| **Equity** | The difference between the value of an asset and the amount owed on that asset; asset value less the debt. |
| **Equity Charge™** | The accumulated capitalised interest on the equity used, over a specified period. |
| **Estate Plan** | A documented plan of how a person's asset will be taken care of after death. A will is part of an estate plan. |
| **Exponentially** | Rapidly increasing (as in size or extent) in an extreme manner. |
| **Fire Sale** | The sale of assets at very low prices, typically when the seller faces bankruptcy. |

| | |
|---|---|
| **Fittings** | Furnishings; items that are added that could be removed. Example: lights or curtain rails. |
| **Fixtures** | In real estate, a piece of the property that is permanently attached. The fixture is considered a part of the property if it shares the same useful life as the rest of the property. Example: kitchen cupboards. |
| **Fringe Benefit** | An incidental advantage; a benefit provided by an employer to supplement an employee's income (such as a company car or living away from home allowance). |
| **Fringe Benefit Tax (FBT)** | The tax paid on a fringe benefit. |
| **Fundamental** | The foundation, the basic requirements. |
| **Gross** | The full amount of profit or salary not including taxes, fees and other expenses. |
| **Income Tax** | Tax paid on income. For an individual it is a progressively increasing amount. For a company it is fixed. |
| **Incur** | Make oneself subject to; bring upon oneself; become liable to. |
| **Index** | A number or ratio derived from a series of observed facts; can reveal relative changes as a function of time: a method of measuring. For example, the index of the stock market is used to determine the overall trend of the market on a daily, weekly or even yearly basis. |
| **Indexed for Inflation** | This means the dollar figure is adjusted for inflation. |

| | |
|---|---|
| **Inflation** | The name given to the change in the value of money. Inflation of 5% per year means your $1.00 is worth only $0.95 at the end of the first year, and only $0.90 after two years. You need to always take into account inflation when choosing an investment vehicle because it helps you determine if your money is going backwards. An economy with 5% inflation requires investments to return at least 6% because at 5% your money is neutral, and anything less is going backwards. |
| **Infrastructure** | The large-scale public systems, services, and facilities of a country or region that are necessary for economic activity, including power and water supplies, public transportation, telecommunications, roads and schools. |
| **Interest Only** | A type of loan where your repayments only cover the interest. |
| **Interest Rates** | The percentage of interest paid on a loan. |
| **Land Tax** | A tax on property imposed by states or territories; usually based on the estimated value of the property. See Office of State Revenue in this glossary for the state websites. |
| **Land Tax Threshold** | The amount of land that can be held free of land tax. It varies from state to state. |
| **Legal Control** | Legal title only. A person with legal control can buy and sell an asset but will never own or enjoy the benefits of ownership (such as income or usage). |
| **Line of Credit** | A pre-approved loan facility that allows the lender to withdraw amounts wherever they desire. Interest is paid only on the total amount withdrawn. |
| **Litigable** | Giving cause for a lawsuit: able to be pursued in court. |
| **Loan to Value Ratio (LVR)** | The loan amount compared to the asset value represented as a percentage. The formula is (loan/asset value) x 100 = LVR % |

| | |
|---|---|
| **Macro** | The bigger picture. (The global economy is a macro outlook compared to the Australian economy.) |
| **Managed Fund** | An investment fund managed for a number of clients by a company, often involving a combination of fixed-interest and property investments at the discretion of the fund managers. |
| **Margin Call** | Margin in this sense refers to the capital or amount invested in shares. A margin call is when the lender requires a capital payment (cash) to maintain the required capital/debt ratio. |
| **Marginal Rate** | The increasing tax rate paid on income as it rises. |
| **Member** | The person entitled to the assets contained in a superannuation fund upon retirement. |
| **Micro** | The small picture. (Your personal micro financial situation compared to the nation's financial situation.) |
| **Mortgage** | A loan from the bank usually used to purchase a house. *Mort* is an Old French word meaning dead, and *gage,* also Old French means a pledge — so, put another way, the word mortgage means a pledge until death! |
| **Necessarily** | Inevitably, essentially. |
| **Net or Nett** | The amount less taxes, fees and all other expenses; remaining after all deductions. |
| **Net Worth** | The different between your assets and liabilities equals your net worth. (Net worth = total assets – total liabilities.) |
| **Onus** | A duty or responsibility; burden. |
| **P&I** | Principal and Interest. A type of loan where your repayment pays the interest and only a small portion of the actual loan amount. |
| **P&L** | Abbreviation for Profit and Loss statement. |
| **Pawn** | A person who is affected by the constant changes in the tax law and does nothing about it. |

| | |
|---|---|
| **Personal Guarantee** | The permission for a financial institution to claim your personal assets and income should the entity which borrowed the money (such as a trust or company) become unable to pay the loan. |
| **Plant** | The equipment and machinery necessary for carrying on a business. For the property investor it relates to such things as dishwashers, ovens, etc. |
| **Player** | A person who understands that property investment is a game, knows the fundamentals of the game and continues to learn more as the rules of the game change. |
| **Principal** | The original amount of a debt on which interest is calculated. |
| **Profit & Loss Statement** | A list of your income and expenses. |
| **Proprietary Limited (Pty Ltd)** | "Proprietary" means relating to an owner or ownership. Proprietary Limited is a type of company whose ownership is limited to a certain number of shares and shareholders. A company that has no restrictions on ownership is normally listed on the stock exchange, where its shares can be purchased by anyone; this is called a Limited type company and will have the abbreviation "Ltd" after its name. |
| **Prudential** | Cautious, careful and considerate. |
| **Quarantined** | Kept separate from something else by force; isolated. |
| **TFN** | Tax File Number — a unique number that assists the government in monitoring and reconciling personal income and taxes. |
| **Third Party Mortgage** | When a loan is guaranteed by the assets of someone other than the person taking out the loan. |
| **Threshold** | A level, or point at which something would happen or cease to happen. |

| | |
|---|---|
| **Trust** | A trust is basically an agreement or promise to hold assets. The basic function of a trust is to separate control and ownership and, as a result, a trust provides asset protection and income distribution flexibility. |
| **Trustee** | The person with legal control who is trusted with the assets and decisions related to a trust or super fund. |
| **Vendor's Finance** | Finance provided by the seller of an asset. |
| **Vested Interest** | A special interest in maintaining or promoting something for personal gain. |
| **Wealth** | An abundance of material possessions and resources. |
| **Yield** | The income from an asset. |

# Player's To-do List

1. ----------

2. ----------

3. ----------

4. ----------

5. ----------

6. ----------

7. ----------

8. ----------

9. ----------

10. ----------

11. ----------

12. ------------------------------------------------------------

13. ------------------------------------------------------------

14. ------------------------------------------------------------

15. ------------------------------------------------------------

16. ------------------------------------------------------------

17. ------------------------------------------------------------

18. ------------------------------------------------------------

19. ------------------------------------------------------------

20. ------------------------------------------------------------

21. ------------------------------------------------------------

22. ------------------------------------------------------------

23. 

24. 

25. 

26. 

27. 

28. 

29. 

30. 

# Caring for your business & family from generation to generation.

Chan & Naylor is a national accounting group ranked in BRW's Top 100 Accountancy Firms in Australia. Established over twenty years ago by Edward Chan and David Naylor, Chan & Naylor was named BRW's fastest-growing accounting practice for three years running — in 2007, 2008 and 2013. We have offices in most major cities — including Melbourne, Sydney, Perth and Brisbane.

The secret of our success is a commitment to service, knowledge and meeting our clients' needs. We are recognised for our cutting-edge and innovative approaches to finding affordable solutions to our clients' challenges.

At Chan & Naylor, you can count on our knowledge in the following areas: tax strategies; small business; property investing; buying property using your self-managed superannuation fund; accounting services; and leading-edge strategies around asset protection and wealth creation — particularly via property investing, estate planning and tax planning.

Chan & Naylor have become one of the country's premier specialist accountants in the area of structuring, and within the firm we have nurtured an expertise that rivals — and even surpasses — some of the largest accountancy firms in Australia. Even partners of the largest accountancy and law firms come to us for their own personal accountancy needs. We prepare tax returns for over 6,000 clients.

Chan & Naylor is the model firm studied by thousands of students when undertaking their CPA studies from the Australian Society of Certified

Practising Accountants and students completing their MBA at Queensland University.

Our motto is "To help our clients increase and protect their net worth from generation to generation".

**Contact us now!**

**Tax-Information registration:**

A **FREE** 15–minute Question and Answer service is provided by Chan & Naylor.

To register your question please go to www.chan-naylor.com.au and complete the enquiry form.

Call us to make an appointment to discuss your tax and accounting requirements or call your local Chan & Naylor office direct. Details are on our website.

**www.chan-naylor.com.au**

Register your details to receive our **FREE** — and most informative — monthly Taxation & Accounting Newsletter

www.ingramcontent.com/pod-product-compliance
Ingram Content Group UK Ltd.
Pitfield, Milton Keynes, MK11 3LW, UK
UKHW020123200726
13856UKWH00002B/696

9 780648 258322